Modern Principles
of
Economic Mechanics

Vol. 1

Modern Principles
of
Economic Mechanics

Volume I

Qualitative Initiatives toward Integrating
Economics, Cognitive Science,
and Theoretical Physics

Yingrui Yang

To order additional copies of this book, contact:
Xlibris Corporation
1-888-795-4274
www.Xlibris.com
Orders@Xlibris.com
109600

Contents

Dedicated to Li,

Who has been with this book from its beginning

Volume I

Scientific Observation,

Quantum Theoretic Principles,

and

the Relativistic Framework Applied

Preface

Currently, economics and cognitive science are heavily rooted in Newtonian physics, successfully borrowing a great deal of modeling tools from it. This is a great achievement. You do not need quantum mechanics or theories of relativity to build a house or bridge. Nevertheless, no one would deny the importance of modern theoretical physics. I believe many intellectuals have realized the need to go beyond the limitations of the Newtonian tradition for means of social science research. The big question is how to do it and how to do it right. For this generation of social scientists, we can update our knowledge-base and training through self-study, while simultaneously familiarizing ourselves with the knowledge of related disciplines. This book aims to integrate economics and cognitive science by applying theoretical physics from a modeling perspective. During the course of this book, necessary background knowledge preparations for understanding the content topics are also briefly provided. I have attempted to write this book similarly to how I teach; I always try to make my lectures conceptually, as well as instrumentally, self-contained.

I wrote down the first principle for this book in 2005. I have been increasingly motivated since then. I decided to start publishing my work along the line presented in this book because I am convinced that the fundamentals of this interdisciplinary framework have been worked out at the basic level or to a considerable amount.

Though a lot of work remains to be done, substantial progress has been made, and it is ready to be communicated with colleagues in different disciplines.

I have lectured on the topics outlined in the introduction (Chapter 0) for the past seven years at Rensselaer Polytechnic Institute. The materials were updated each semester as new ideas were developed. My students had no textbook, and I kept making promises to them about my book. Over the years, during summer and winter breaks, I gave talks on selected topics presented in this book at a number of Chinese universities, including Tsinghua University, Peking University, People's University of China, Beijing Normal University, Sun Yi-Sian University, and the Institute of Psychology (Chinese Academy of Science). The audiences demanded further readings, and I kept making promises about my book to them as well. It may take me another year to complete the rest of the book. Thus, I decided to divide the book into three volumes and publish the Volume I first as it is now. Volume II and Volume III are also outlined in detail in introductory Chapter 0 of the present volume and both Volumes II and III are planned to be available in 2013.

This book is self-published through Xlibris, as book proposals were declined without external review by six top university presses sequentially. By his own view, the present author evaluates this work as going to be one of the most important contributions to basic theoretical research in social sciences during the early twenty-first century and predicts the work along this line to be a potential candidate for a possible Nobel Prize in Economic Sciences in the years to come. I offer an open invitation to colleagues from various academic communities and backgrounds worldwide to offer critical peer reviews. Meanwhile, I can only hope colleagues from related disciplines who become interested in the research along this line to join the effort.

English is not my native language. The students in my classes all helped me to polish my writing for several rounds. Particularly, Alexander Bringsjord, Scott Carpman, Nathan Nardino, and Casey Pham edited and polished my writing through the whole volume. Tyler Convery prepared the figures and the cover page for me. My colleagues Prof. Selmer Bringsjord, Prof. Jim Fahey, and Prof. Michael Zenzen carefully edited and polished Chapter 1, Chapter 5, and Chapter 6, respectively. My department chair, Professor Bringsjord, has paid close attention to the progress of my work; without his understanding about academic freedom and his support to basic theoretical research, my journey would be much more difficult. This work was partly supported by the Wei-Lun Special Professorship of Tsinghua University during my sabbatical (2007–2008). Prof. Xiaojun Wang participated in my seminar at Tsinghua University and had many suggestive discussions with me over years. Prof. Zhengxing Wang, who taught theoretical physics for over fifty years at Peking University, met with me and talked with me over the phone to answer my questions patiently. All helped. I thank each of them wholeheartedly.

Chapter 0

Introduction—Outlines of the Book (Volumes I–III)

In preparing this book, the present author has utilized two sets of books in mind for key background models and sample references. One set consists of a number of classic masterpieces, which establish principles in their chosen domain. These are William James (1900), Whitehead & Russell (1910/1927), Alfred Marshall (1926), and Paul Dirac (1930). The early twentieth century was a time for these great thinkers to set up the foundations for their chosen disciplines. Sciences in the twenty-first century are going to be highly interdisciplinary. The work presented in this book aims to build some cornerstones for the integration of economics, cognitive science, and theoretical physics (beyond Newtonian mechanics).

The other set includes a number of popular advanced scientific books, which I have tried to follow stylistically. It includes volumes by Albert Einstein, Stephen Hawking, Roger Penrose, Douglas Hofstadter, John Searle, Frank Wilczek, Milton Friedman, Friedrich August von Hayek, Ludwig von Mises, Brian Greene, Richard Feynman, Georg Simmel, David McMahon, Anthony Zee, Martinus Veltman, Lisa Randall, etc. They are all artists in compiling materials to create advanced, but not specialized, scientific books. Since the main focus of this book is on the integration of three disciplines, this book does not intend to serve as an introduction to any particular domain. Accordingly, only the necessary and essential materials from each domain are carefully selected and adjusted to illustrate the integrations that have been worked out. Extra material from one domain would require additional materials from other domains accordingly and would demand further integrations to be worked out. Thus, this extra material would be beyond the scope of the present book.

The new contributions in this book can be viewed along three lines. First, there are three major sub-domains in higher cognitive research: reasoning, decision making, and behavioral game theory, each of which has been previously studied independently. One of the reasons for this separation was that each sub-domain is under a different normative theory (i.e., logic, modern axiomatic decision theory, and game theory). These are integrated from formal as well as empirical perspectives in this volume. Second, economics and cognitive science share two normative theories as standard languages, namely, decision theory and game theory. However, a great deal of empirical phenomena have been discovered which cannot be explained by decision theory and game theory alone. What has been overlooked in economics is logic and human reasoning at the sub-economic level. The work presented in this volume provides new mechanisms to enable us to look into reasoning processes underlying decision making and game theoretic interactions. Third, both current cognitive science and modern economics are conceptually and mathematically rooted in classical Newtonian mechanics. The integration here demands conceptual insights and mathematical tools used in modern theoretical physics including quantum theory, theories of relativity, and quantum field theory (e.g., quantum chromodynamics and quantum electrodynamics).

contextual

This book argues that human economy is, by nature, experimental and proposes a new framework that goes beyond the Newtonian tradition of psychophysics and econophysics by applying quantum theoretic, as well as relativistic principles. These three lines of thinking are integrated through careful arguments, thorough mathematical and formal treatments, and analogical conceptual transformations, starting from physics leading to the initial integration of economics and cognitive science.

The outlines below serve as a map to the structure of the book. The book is divided into three volumes containing a total of nineteen chapters. Volume I: Scientific Observations, Quantum Theoretic Principles, and Relativistic Framework Applied, consists of the present chapter, and Chapters 1–6. Volume II: Three Levels of Integrations: From Cognition and Economics to Standard Model in Theoretical Physics, consists of Chapters 7–11. Volume III: Quantum Field Theoretic Modeling, consists of Chapters 12–18. Though the present volume contains only Chapters 0–6, in order for readers to have some overall ideas about the entire book, the outline for each of the eighteen chapters across three volumes will be provided in the rest of this chapter.

0.1 *The Detailed Outline of Volume I: Scientific Observations, Quantum Theoretic Principles, and Relativity Framework Applied*

This volume first sets up the basis for a new approach to integrate cognitive science, economics, and theoretical physics. Chapter 1 makes an ontological commitment to what Whitehead calls "the experimental world." This view allows us to classify the observations of the physical world, the mental world, and the economic world in terms of the degree of disturbance. When the degree of disturbance is high, quantum theory shall apply. Chapter 2 raises several logical and mathematical issues in the foundation of modern consumption theory. The notion of modal revealed preference is introduced to model the potential consumer. Along that line, eleven quantum theoretic principles, four in Chapter 1 and seven in Chapter 2, are postulated. It then applies the special and general theories of relativity to the integration of cognitive science and economics. Chapters 3–5 are about the special theory of relativity and monetary analysis. Chapter 6 is about the general theory of relativity and economic space that is filled with a field of mental ethers. Chapters 3 and 4 make progress in steps to argue that money, in analogy to light, travels in economic world with the highest and constant speed. Chapter 5 introduces the economic space-time and explores the money cone. Chapter 6 introduces the notion of a curved economic space, then defines the Pareto efficiency in terms of geodesics in the general theory of relativity and defines economic gravity in terms of curvature (i.e., possible Pareto improvement).

Chapter 1 Principles Concerning the Directedness of Observation

The key concepts introduced in this chapter are the directions of observation and correspondingly the degree of disturbance of scientific observations in physical, mental, and economic worlds. This crucial idea is called the orthogonal law. In Sections 1.1–1.3, the following four principles are postulated and discussed:

Principle 1   (*orthogonal observational directions*) Scientific
                 observations are directional. The inward observation
                 of the mental world and the outward observation

of the physical world are in opposite observational directions.

Principle 2   (*the disturbance principle*) The higher the degree of disturbance in the experiment, the smaller the world that can be observed (Dirac).

Principle 3   (*the diagonal law*) Experiments of higher-order cognition and experiments of quantum physics are in the same spectrum of the "Yes/No" type experimentation (von Neumann; Penrose, 2004), and they both share a great deal of the same family of mathematical branches.

Principle 4   (*the economy principle*) Human economy is, by nature, experimental. It involves backward observation (using the historical data) and forward observation. Forward observation is of the Yes/No type experimentation.

We distinguish the "Yes/No" type experiments from the "Smooth" type of experiments and show why different branches of mathematics follow, respectively, from modeling perspectives. Section 1.4 discusses the relation of non-observables and symmetry. It establishes the symmetries between observations trying to zoom in on the physical world, mental world, and economic world.

Chapter 2 Principles Concerned with New Economic Mechanics

Section 2.1   argues cognitive science and economics are naturally related neighboring fields. Higher-order cognitive research shares two normative theories with modern economics, namely, modern axiomatic decision theory and game theory. What has been overlooked is the relation between logic and decision theory. We show that the meta-property in decision theory, the representation theorem, can be seen as decision theoretic completeness and consistency and is parallel to the meta-properties of standard formal logic. These normative theories are treated as gauge theories that possess the internal structure referred to as "isospin" between syntactic components and semantic components, both of which carry logic charge but with differing signs. Three clusters of symmetries are defined accordingly from observation perspectives. The notion of logic charge has an important application in Chapters 13 and 14.

Section 2.2   defines the concept of economic rationality (or, the economically rational man) via four requirements with regard to the decision theoretic structure. It explains why and how the notion of economic rationality is used to characterize the personified, ideal market itself, but not any individual market participants. In Volumes II and III, we will explain that logic, modern decision theory, game theory, and the neoclassical economics, which are all centered on economic rationality and general equilibrium. These theories should be treated as gauge theories with global symmetries based on null observations; these gauge theories define the economic and sub-economic stationary states. When psychological or behavioral research involving non-null observations are taken into account, the global symmetries of these gauge theories undergo what is referred to in quantum field theory as spontaneous breaking.

Section 2.3   explains why a certain degree of invisibility of a market is necessary in order for a fair market to keep all the observations of individual participants symmetrical. Four different kinds of possible invisible hands are characterized: Newtonian, special relativistic, general relativistic, and quantum invisible hands. The symmetry associated with each possible invisible hand is discussed from observational perspectives.

Section 2.4   points out that the current consumption theories start from the "n" goods and all the possible combinations (bundles) of these n goods. All of the literature in economics, particularly the textbooks, never tells us whether n is finite or infinite. We distinguish the two cases and show that different logical and mathematical analyses follow each case. We then explain why this is sensitive to the observations of individual market participants.

Section 2.5   introduces the notion of modal revealed preference. Samuelson's revealed preference from its original set theoretic description is reformulated into possible world semantics (i.e., the semantics used in modal logic) and redefined as modal revealed preference. It can be used to characterize potential consumers and potential markets. Along these lines, seven quantum theoretic principles are postulated. For example, after introducing modal revealed preference and potential market, the so-called first principle in quantum mechanics by Hilbert is given as: "The real potentiality is the squared possibility." This principle follows a real world example in financial crisis.

Chapter 3   A Threefold "Isospin" of Money, Consciousness, and Light

This chapter aims to establish isospin, a special symmetry among light consciousness, and money. As Zee (1986/2007) described, Heisenberg's symmetry is called isospin. Inspired by rotational symmetry, Heisenberg postulated that the proton may be rotated into the neutron and *vice versa*. For example, one observer sees a proton, but another observer, whose viewpoint is isospin rotated from the first, may insist that a neutron is seen. In our particular discussion of integration, when we refer to isospin, it means that if we rotate the fields from the physical world to the economic world or to the mental world, what we initially saw as the light would now be viewed as money or consciousness, respectively. In other words, they are agents belonging to the same agency. They are assigned to different fields to perform almost the same kind of duties.

Section 3.1   introduces a number of properties of light in terms of its mass, energy, and speed. Together, we collectively call these properties the family of "light-like-ness." Section 3.2 provides a new way to consider the "quasi-light-ness" of consciousness. Consciousness as a mental state is traditionally associated with other properties of the mind such as subjectivity, intentionality, and causality (Searle,

1984). Strategically, we first isolate the state of being conscious from other mental states and enable it to travel in the mental world at the highest speed. We argue that consciousness is 'content-less', which is a distinctly unique mental state due to its very intrinsic physical orientation. Thus, being conscious can be characterized by a quantum theoretic vector, which has a direction and has no length. Consciousness is characterized by mental gluons, which are responsible for bounding impulses at the sub-economic level.

Section 3.3   uses the same analogy. People developed their concept about money from learning about its functional powers such as purchasing power, saving power, and investing power. However, when one says, "I just need to make more money," money has achieved an independent status, distinctly secular from its functional powers. In this way, money is said to be "massless." Consequently, this makes it possible for money to travel with the highest speed in a given space, where the functional powers (originally attached to money) serve as the spatial dimensions. The former statement can also be viewed in the cognitive or economic sense. If we view economics in terms of the special theory of relativity, every economic thing travels with the same combined speed in "economic space-time," but money does not divert any combined speed to the time dimension. In an adaptation of Green's words (1999), it can be said that "money never wastes any time." This chapter is the first step toward applying the special theory of relativity to monetary analysis.

Chapter 4 The Quasi-light-ness (Energy and Speed) of Money

This chapter contains a great deal of literature reviews. Section 4.1 is largely based on Simmel's classic work, *Philosophy of Money* (1990). Poggi (1993) summarized twelve properties of money and grouped them into four clusters. A number of remarks are made to support the claim that money is always in motion: it transfers mental energy to economic energy, it transforms human intelligence into economic activities, and it is "massless" in terms of commodity. Money is the logical relation of all commodities and of all individuals, and therefore, "money is in constant motion" (Simmel, 1990). Notice that most of these remarks are sociologically centered.

In Section 4.2, several controversies in monetary analysis are reviewed: whether money is dimensional or adimensional (dimensionless), whether money is neutral (e.g., Lucas; Friedman) or never neutral (e.g., von Mises), and the debates between the Keynesian approach and the Austrian school of economic thought (e.g., von Mises; Hayek). Along these lines, remarks are made on each controversial topic, stating that money is adimensional, that money travels faster than any other economic event, and that money travels with a limited speed due to the fact that modern money has a unique intrinsic value, nationality (disputing the notion of "denationalization" of money, Hayek, 1976). This chapter serves as the second step to prepare us for applying the special theory of relativity to monetary analysis.

Chapter 5   Money and the Special Theory of Relativity

Section 5.1   reviews the controversy between the banking school and the monetary school ways of monetary analysis, concerning the relation between price and money supply. We consider the notion of money emission by Schmitt (1982) and Cencini (1988). Dirac's δ-function is then introduced and used to characterize money emission. Furthermore, we apply a well-known property of the δ-function, namely: $\int_{-\infty}^{\infty} f(x)\delta(x)dx = f(x_0)$, where we let $f(x)$ be a continuous pricing function. The end result is particularly interesting and natural. The meaning of this result is discussed.

Section 5.2   is about the denial of what Wilczek (2008) called Newton's Zeroth Law, which states that "mass is neither created nor destroyed." In *The Lightness of Being*, Wilczek proposes that energy is more likely to be the origin of matter rather than mass. Here, we introduce an economic version of the Newtonian Zeroth Law in terms of real materialistic productions, and then apply Wilczek's idea to discuss money and the mental energy money inherently carries.

Lastly, in Section 5.3, we construct a four-dimensional Minkowski space-time, of which three monetary functions (purchasing, saving, and investing) serve as three spatial dimensions. Time serves as the fourth dimension (or it can multiply the monetary speed to create the energy dimension). In the special theory of relativity, each coordinate basis represents a different individual admissible observer. Thus, when the Lorentz transformation is introduced, all the admissible market participants observe the same monetary law. We then introduce the notion of intervals and explain what we mean by the "money cone." The money cone displays the causal relations of time-like economic events for a given money emission.

Chapter 6   Mental Ethers, Pareto Efficiency,
                    and Economic Gravity

In the previous chapter, the special theory of relativity was applied and the Minkowski space-time was defined as flat. In this chapter, the general theory of relativity will be applied and economic space-time will be curved, rather than flat. In Section 6.1, we assume that among people, individuals may have different ideas and pay varying amounts of attention to a given economic event, and each particular individual may have different ideas and pay varying amount of attention from one event to another. Thus, taking the insight from Wilczek, we will introduce the notion of mental ethers as space filling things, and we assume that the distribution of mental ethers is aeolotropic everywhere in the economic space-time.

Section 6.2   introduces   the   notion   of   what   we   call
                    macro-externality. Externality is traditionally a
                    concept in microeconomics because it is related to
                    particular trading. Here, we treat financial policies
                    as tradings, and the price can be extremely high
                    (such as the $700 billion bailout). It causes different
                    externalities to individuals (e.g., tax payers), which
                    forms an aeolotropic distribution. In the above sense,

we say that a cognitive aeolotropic field is attached to economic space-time.

Sections 6.3–6.5 are a bit more technical. Section 6.3 shows why tensor analysis is required from a modeling perspective. We introduce the notion of economic polarization (analogous to the polarization of an electronic field) between a policy stimuli vector and a market response vector. When the field is aeolotropic, economic polarization is characterized by a tensor. The notion of a tensor is introduced in some detail (but kept at a minimum) to make the descriptions self-sufficient.

Section 6.4   introduces the notion of local curvilinear coordinates. Not only is this a necessary mathematical tool used in the general theory of relativity, but also allows for each coordinate basis to stand for a market observer. The curved frame of local coordinates is also described in some detail (but also kept at a minimum) to make the descriptions self-sufficient.

After the above preparations, Section 6.5 introduces the notion of Pareto efficiency in economics and the notion of geodesics in the general theory of relativity. A mathematical treatment (where all isovectors, termed "null tangent vectors" are parallel) is used to define the Pareto-efficient state as the economic geodesics. Accordingly, the notion of economic curvature is defined as the difference (i.e., possible Pareto improvements) between the Pareto-geodesics and a real economic state, which in turn defines "economic gravity." This model entails that all the market observers (represented by a local coordinate basis) are in accelerated frames from economics perspectives, according to the Einstein principle of general relativity.

0.2 *The Detailed Outline of Volume II: From Economics and Cognition to the Standard Model in Theoretical Physics*

This volume involves three levels of integrations, all of which are subsequently characterized. At the first level, three formalisms (also called normative theories or standard theories related to cognitive and economic modeling) are introduced: formal logic, modern axiomatic decision theory, and game theory (Chapters 7 and 8). We show why it is necessary and how to integrate the three formalisms by establishing a transformation mechanism (Chapter 9). In order to account for the empirical research, the bra-ket formalism of quantum theory by Dirac is also introduced (Chapter 8). This volume is not designed as a course of any one normative theory in particular, but rather a minimal introduction of the conceptual structure of each theory to provide the necessary but self-sufficient language for reading the subsequent material within this volume. All the normative theories are introduced in a special way, such that for each theory, we make clear distinctions between theoretical syntax, semantics, and meta-properties. This unified treatment allows for the transformations between formalisms to take place. There are many misunderstandings, and therefore, many controversies about why we need normative theories and what roles they play in cognitive science and economic empirical research. A number of remarks are made to clarify these issues.

At the second level, psychological theories and models in higher-order cognitive research, which are closely related to economic modeling, are summarized (Chapter 10). We then characterize experimentation, from a quantum theoretic perspective, in subject areas such as the psychology of reasoning, decision making and judgment, and behavioral game theory. More attention is given to the psychology of reasoning as it was the present author's primary research domain through the 1990s. The central debates between major competing theories in reasoning and in decision making are briefly reviewed (e.g., Psychological Review, 1994; 1996). We show how and why quantum theory provides the necessary conceptual ideas and mathematical tools to address the challenges from both empirical and modeling perspectives (Chapter 11). The key quantum theoretic concepts are discussed: quantum fluctuation, degree of disturbance, "spun" of stimuli, eigenvalues and eigenstates, noncommutative operators, projection principle, wave function, amplitude, and complex field semantics.

At the third level, we integrate the above two levels of integrations (so it can be seen as meta-integration). This is done by introducing quantum field theoretic concepts in steps during the modeling process (Chapters 7–11). This approach allows us to move slowly but naturally toward an unprecedented, qualitative modification of the standard model (in theoretical physics) for means of integrating economics and cognitive science (summarized in Chapter 11). The standard model of particle physics was originally proposed by C.N. Yang and R.L. Mills (1954), so it is also known as Yang-Mills theory. More quantum field theoretic concepts (e.g., creation and annihilation) and modeling work will be provided in Volume III as well. These key concepts discussed are: gauge theory, global symmetry, spontaneous symmetry breaking, local symmetry, null observation, stationary state, boson particle and force carrier, basis state, vacuum and expected value, Higgs field, degenerated state, accelerated state, gauge transformation, phase space, and Higgs mechanism.

Chapter 7 Conceptual Framework of Modern Logic

Section 7.1   discusses the need for normative theories. Section
               7.2 is the only section that spells out the details of
               a formal system: propositional logic. This provides
               readers with a clear idea of the three standard
               components in a logical system: formal syntax,
               formal semantics, and meta-properties. Taken
               together, the consistency and the completeness of
               this logical system showcase the beautiful symmetry
               contained within it. Also mentioned in this section
               are Jeffrey's "logic of decision" and the weaknesses
               associated with it.

Section 7.3   provides remarks on formalism to clarify a number
               of misunderstandings toward normative theories.
               Section 7.4 introduces quantified predicate logic
               and its value-assignment semantics. Based on my
               teaching experience, it is contextually agreeable to
               keep this section brief but thorough for the purpose
               of conveying a basic understanding without diving
               into meticulous detail. Here, we also point out
               why predicate logic is important in studying the
               reasoning processes underlying decision making.
               Section 7.5 introduces modal operators and possible
               world semantics. Particular emphasis is placed on
               the canonical method for constructing different
               individual domains on possible worlds. As previously
               mentioned in Chapter 2, modal logic is a powerful
               formalism which can be used to model the potential
               market.

Four principle points are declared. First, normative theories (such as logic, decision theory, and game theory) can be viewed as gauge theories. They are tools (or extended rulers) scientists have developed to gauge mental activities or economic phenomenon. Second, from an experimental viewpoint, it is imperative to treat gauge theories as being paired with null observations. Gauge theories should be paired with null observations because the gauged activities (mental or economic) have not yet been performed. At this point of integration, it should be realized that gauge theories enable us to define the so-called stationary states in sub-economic (mental) and economic worlds. Third, we say the mental and economic activities (termed "elements") defined by gauge theories are all "massless" (no experience, no cost). Fourth, the technical languages used in gauge theories about the mind and economy have innate internal structures which help us to identify various elements. To better understand these elements, their functionality can be viewed as intrinsic force carriers, serving as mental (sub-economic) or economic forces (energies not forces, actually). Without making the ontological commitment to sub-economic and economic forces, it would be difficult to model subsequent interactions.

Chapter 8   Decision Theory, Game Theory, and Quantum Theory

Section 8.1   introduces the conceptual architecture of modern axiomatic decision theory. It includes decision theoretic syntax, utility semantics, and the representation theorem, which is the meta-property that represents the internal symmetry within a decision system. Also discussed is the difference between the Platonic tradition of "knowing" and Wittgenstein's idea about "doing." Then we introduce more modern versions of decision theoretic syntax based on action functions and state variables. The debate between two major competing approaches, causal decision theory and referential decision theory, is briefly described and a resolution proposed by Joyce (1999) is discussed.

Section 8.2   introduces the so-called Nash framework of game theory, in particular, the distinction between noncooperative and cooperative games. We explain why the Nash framework is an important contribution, when considering Wittgenstein's idea about the language game. The game theoretic syntax, the benefit semantics (based on value sets and strategies), and the Nash equilibrium as the meta-property for noncooperative games are all described. We show why cooperative games are usually defined in a purely semantic way in terms of a set of agreements and describe the Nash solution as the meta-property. Both the Nash equilibrium and the Nash solution show symmetries within the game theoretic framework.

Section 8.3   introduces a very general quantum theoretic syntax, namely, Dirac's bra-ket formalism and its modified Feynman version. Through this syntax, we explain how quantum theory is probably the only formalism designed to characterize experimental procedures, thus it is a crucial formalism to the framework represented in this volume. The field of complex numbers is introduced as the quantum theoretic semantics for the Dirac formalism, and an explanation for its necessity is provided from an experimental perspective. The notion of stimuli spin in the mental world and economic world is also introduced, which explains why the quantum theoretic semantics need to have both real and the imaginative terms. We discussed what the "i" and the "θ" terms in an exponential format of a complex number stand for from economic and cognitive perspectives. A brief explanation about how this approach works is provided in the following.

Let us consider an example in reasoning: from a set of premises: ($p{\rightarrow}q$), ($q{\rightarrow}r$), and p, one can infer r. By Feynman (1989)'s usage of Dirac's bra-ket formalism, the inference above can be represented as:

$$\langle r \,|q, q \rightarrow r\rangle \langle q \,|p, p \rightarrow q\rangle$$

This representation shows an inference with two steps: $\langle q \,|p, p \rightarrow q\rangle$ first and $\langle r \,|q, q \rightarrow r\rangle$ second. In the first step, it combines two state-vectors: the initial state, $|p, p \rightarrow q\rangle$ (also called a right state vector or a *ket-vector*), and the final (or arrival) state, $\langle r|$ (also called a left state vector or a *bra-vector*). This combination defines the inner product of two state vectors. A quantum theoretic state vector $\langle x|$ or $|x\rangle$ only indicates a direction; it has no length and thus is different from the classical notion of a vector in mathematics. There is a slogan saying that you can put everything you know in the ket. I will explain why it is so shortly. The example above only shows how Dirac's bra-ket notation can be used to represent a logical inference from the syntactic perspective. Similar to a formal logic system, the Dirac formalism also carries logical charge, meaning that it consists of two standard components: the formal syntax and its symbol-theoretic (or number-theoretic) semantics.

The quantum theoretic semantics for Dirac's bra-ket syntax is the field of complex number. The quantum theoretic meaning of each single bra-ket inner product has to be determined, or say, to be assigned by a complex number. The following is one way to illustrate this determining (assignment) mechanism.

Different from other formal systems, the Dirac formalism is designed to characterize the virtual quantum theoretic experimentation. Here, by virtual, it means prior to actual measurement conducted; this virtuality can be seen as characterized by the imaginary number i. The virtual experiment is modeled to make predictions for potential probability, which must be a real number to be determined by a real measurement. Now let us consider a virtual experiment in general. Assume that an experimental item was constructed and a sample of participants selected. Write the item state vector as a ket-vector $|item\rangle$ and the sample state vector as a bra-vector $\langle sample|$. To combine the two, we can have the bra-ket inner product $\langle sample|item\rangle$. By some authors, it can be read as to run an experiment on the item by testing the sample of randomly selected participants. In the more standard explanation, we may first assume the bra-vector $\langle sample|$ is normalized (i.e., $\langle A|A\rangle =1$). Then $\langle sample|item\rangle$ can be seen as the *projection* of $|item\rangle$ on the direction of $\langle sample|$, written as: *item*(*sample*), which is called the *wave function* of the state, $|item\rangle$, on the direction of $\langle sample|$. Here the measurable quantity is the accuracy; in this case, say the statistical result of accuracy at this point is a.

One might think what is described above is just a simple case in psychology of reasoning. Why do we need to consult a complex formalism in modeling? If we take into account the possible complex structure of a psychological experiment, we may understand better about the modeling power of Dirac's bra-ket formalism. Assume the above virtual experiment is given in English, using the English version of the verbal item and native English speakers as subjects. Now we assume the sample and the item *spin*: for example, a strict Chinese version of this experiment can be re-conducted in a cross-language reliability test. Surpose the resulting accuracy is **b**. Due to the fact that the accuracy information (referred to *i*), **a** as well as **b,** is collected by the experimenter (referred to *I*)**,** who subjectively designed the experiment**,** the meaning of this virtual experiment, ⟨*sample*|*item*⟩, is determined by a complex number, **a+ib**.

The actual experiments can be more complex than what is described above. On one hand, many possible versions (in different languages) of the original experiment can be conducted. On the other hand, we rarely use a single experimental item; instead, a set of testing items (of the same type or compound) is necessary for many experiments. Ideally, a systematically designed set of items would minimize possible noises in the data. In addition, the same experiment can be re-conducted at a different time. To take all of these factors into account, as the meaning of a particular ⟨*sample*|*item*⟩, a specific complex number, **a+ib**, is called the *probability amplitude* of the corresponding wave faction, *Item*(*sample*), which stands only for one possibility. As a metaproperty in general, the squared absolute value of this amplitude is used to predict the real probability obtained from the real experiment (i.e., real measurement).

Let us see one more instance of the bra-ket representation, ⟨*item2*|*item1*⟩. Here *item2* can be seen as an exercise problem in the textbook one studied in preparing for an exam, and *item1* stands for a test problem in the exam. The wave function, *item1*(*item2*), of ⟨*item2*|*item1*⟩ is the projection of *item1* on the diction of *item2*. Now suppose that the average score of one group of students is **a** and that of another group is **b**, then the amplitude of the wave function, *item1*(*item2*), in this particular pairwise possibility is *a+ib*. The exponential form of this complex number would be $re^{i\theta}$, where the phase θ may indicate the difference between two groups. Briefly speaking, a bra-ket form represents the interaction of two possible states.

The observable in the above example is the accuracy. The observables in quantum mechanics are treated as operators. By treating the accuracy as an operator it means that the accuracy can be applied to and measured from any given experiment of the above kind. Another pair of key concepts is eigenvalue and eigenstate. For example, in a reasoning experiment, the subject is asked to answer if a conclusion follows a set of premises given by marking "Yes" or "No", which is called the evaluation test. It would not make sense to ask if the putative conclusion is morally correct or affordable to buy, which are not eigen-questions in this context. When the right question is asked, we have two eigenvalues here: *Yes* or *No*. To count them as eigenvalues, the theory assumes two corresponding mental eigenstates in the cognitive system, namely: |yes⟩ and |no⟩, given the context. In other words, the individual minds understand what they are responding to. In order to respond to an eigen-question, the eigenvalue must be entangled with the corresponding eigenstate by performing an inference as the stimulus. A good valid stimulus is supposed to be capable of getting into the system, finding the target eigenstate, and entangling it with the corresponding eigenvalue; at this point, we say the original phenomenon logical world collapse. A more technical introduction of Dirac's formalism will be provided in the book (Volum II). A deeper analysis for applying quantum theoretic model to the empirical study in cognitive science and economics will be developed in Chapter 11 (Volume II).

This chapter is the appropriate place to introduce the notion of global symmetry (also see Chapter 2 for the distinction between internal structural global symmetry and external global symmetry with null observations). All the meta-properties within normative theories are characterized by universally quantified statements, such as soundness and completeness of logic systems, representational theorem of decision theory, and Nash equilibrium (noncooperative) or Nash solution (cooperative) of game theory. Thus, each of these gauge theories possesses a kind of global symmetry. Symmetry and symmetry breaking are crucial concepts in the development of modern theoretical physics (Zee, 1986/1999). Mainzer (2005) introduced these tools to economic and social analyses but mostly in terms of equilibrium from game theoretic perspectives. In the next chapter, we will see why this is simply not enough for the integrative manipulations we seek to achieve. Additionally, the concept of spontaneous breaking will be introduced in Chapter 10, where empirical studies are taken into account.

Chapter 9 Mental Decision Logic

This chapter establishes symmetries among game theory, decision theory, and mental predicate logic (Braine, 1998) through new formal transformations. Sections 9.1 and 9.2 represent some extended work of Yang (2006). Here, we regard game theory as a communication language, decision making as a public language in terms of actions, and reasoning as a private language that is purely mental. Empirical research in behavioral game theory has revealed a great deal of robust phenomena that requires explanations from individual decision-making perspectives (e.g., Camerer, 1999). Still, many phenomena reported in the psychology of decision making demand an investigation of the reasoning process that underlies decision making. Nonetheless, to construct a formal model accounting for this cross-domain process is challenging because it needs to cross the barrier between normative theories.

Section 9.1   also provides a bidirectional formal mechanism, which allows transformations between game theoretic syntax, decision theoretic syntax, and mental predicate logic (to be introduced in more details in Chapter 10). This mechanism can be briefly coded as: $(a_i, a_{-i}) \rightarrow a_i(a_{-i}) \rightarrow f(s) \rightarrow A(x), x \in X$, and is briefly explained by the table below.

Game format	Transformation	Decision format	Logic format	Mental logic
(a_i, a_{-i})	$a_i(a_{-i})$	$f(s)$	$A(x)$	$A(x), x \in X$

Savage (1954) distinguishes between the Stage 1 and the Stage 2 decision processes, and then proposes an open problem called the "small-grand world problem" (SGWP). Section 9.2 provides a formal language and a psychological program toward a solution of the SGWP. From the meta-theoretic perspectives, we also show mathematically that this formal language no longer satisfies Boolean algebra but instead satisfies a ring-ideal structure. Section 9.3 summarizes a qualitative channel theoretic formalism of the SGWP, based on a recently published work (Allwein, Yang, & Harrison, 2011).

Chapter 10   Psychological Theories and Empirical Evidences

Section 10.1 briefly introduces two major competing approaches in the psychology of reasoning: the mental logic theory (e.g., Braine & O'Brien, 1998) and the mental models theory (e.g., Johnson-Laird & Byrne, 1991). Special attention is given to predicate reasoning with quantifiers. We show some characteristics of mental predicate logic (Braine, 1998) and its empirical justifications (Yang, Braine, & O'Brien, 1998). Here, we point out a clear distinction between standard predicate logic and mental predicate logic. In standard predicate logic, formal syntax and formal semantics are formulated separately. For example, $A(x)$ represents a monadic predicate-argument structure in formal syntax, while $x \in X$ represents the truth condition for the predicate "A" in formal semantics. This is because standard predicate logic is domain general. However, the mental predicate logic by Braine (1998) is domain specific. For any predicate-argument structure $A(x)$, a specific individual domain must be identified for individual variable x, formally written as $A(x)$, $x \in X$. This characteristic is justified by the definite article *the* in English. From a modeling perspective, this characteristic converts human thinking into what we would call "local symmetry." Using the definite article *the* is a commonly shared cognitive capacity among most of us, but it means different things from one individual to another. The importance of this idea will be seen after introducing the notion of spontaneous symmetry breaking in Chapter 11.

Additionally, we show illusory reasoning with quantifiers (as predicted by the mental models theory) and its empirical evidence (e.g., Yang & Johnson-Laird, 2000). Here, a careful comparison of the empirical methods used in mental logic experiments and mental models experiments is provided through sample data sets.

Section 10.2 introduces the psychology of judgment and decision making through a debate under the umbrella of bounded rationality, first proposed by Simon (Nobel Laureate in Economics, 1978). The debate is between prospect theory (led by Kahneman, Nobel Laureate in Economics, 2002, and the late Tversky) and a theory based on experience and cues (led by Gerd Gigerenzer). Relations between cognitive "norms" and learning from experience are discussed from an empirical perspective. In Chapter 15, we will review the notion of bounded rationality from more conceptual perspectives.

Section 10.3 reviews behavioral game theory (e.g., Camerer, 1999), which is a fast growing sub-domain that is comprised of economics, management, and cognitive science. We generate what we call the crossing phenomena between noncooperative and cooperative games. The entropy analysis about game theoretic strategies is also discussed. The review summarizes the limitations of the current model of behavioral methods being used in the field.

Section 10.4 addresses a number of general empirical and theoretical issues in higher cognitive research, based on the ideas of mental metalogic (Yang & Bringsjord, 2003; Yang, etc., 2004) and mental decision logic

(Yang, 2006). The notion of "problem types" is introduced. Two meta-theoretical properties, empirical consistency and cognitive completeness, are defined. The significant empirical issue pertains to how single competing theories can account for compound experimental tasks involving more than one item type. This presents a difficult challenge for current psychological and economic theories. The notion of trivial symmetry breaking borrowed from physics will be introduced here. We will illustrate that current psychological and behavioral theories have taken a trivial symmetry breaking approach from theorizing as well as modeling perspectives.

Chapter 11 Experimental Issues and Quantum Theoretic Responses

aka contextualized social si behavior

The key concept for this chapter, and indeed for the whole volume, is experimentation. Section 11.1 extends the set of empirical issues given in Section 10.4 to include more generalized empirical issues by viewing human economy as a family of experiments, per se. There is a distinction between the approach of treating human economy as a family of experiments and what is currently called experimental economics. The latter pertains to running experiments to simulate economic events, while the former pertains to modeling the economy as an experiment and treating individual market participants and policy makers as observers. For example, in current experimental economics, researchers run experiments to simulate and modify how a policy works. In the present proposed framework, it is assumed that the policy maker uses the policy as the stimuli to test the market. In other words, this can be seen as the economics of an experimental economy. We can then discuss experimental issues in both cognitive science and economics while using quantum theoretic language.

To extend the principles postulated in Chapters 1 and 2, Section 11.2 explains a number of results which apply quantum theoretical concepts and methods in order to deal with experimental issues addressed in previous sections. The following is a short list of quantum theoretic topics to be discussed:

i. Mental states and economic states follow superposition law but not addition law.

ii. Raw data sets need to be treated as distributions, which can be seen as probability waves when the degree of disturbance is high in the experiment.

iii. The sample means based on previous data sets should be treated as amplitudes of possibilities in order to calculate the real potentiality (probability) by using the so-called first principle of quantum mechanics (named after Hilbert), when compound experimental items are used.

iv. It is the stimuli (e.g., a SAT item or a fiscal policy), but neither the mind nor the economy, that is spun in terms of spin.

v. The field of complex numbers and complex functional analysis are necessary and powerful when spin is taken into account.

vi. In higher-order cognitive research and in experimental economics, we usually only have two eigenvalues: Yes or No. However, an eigenstate may be a degenerate state (the notion of a degenerate state is explained and applied in Chapter 15 where the principles of ordinary rationality are discussed).

vii. Once an experimental stimulus becomes entangled with the targeted mental or economic states, the original phenomenological world must collapse.

Section 11.3   explains what we mean by the Yes/No type experimentation and why general functional analysis is necessary in cognitive science and economics. Section 11.4 describes the U-R process proposed by Penrose (2004) and how it is a powerful formalism to cognitive and economic modeling. Section 11.5 briefly introduces the Hilbert dual space framework and explains why observables are treated as operators. Section 11.6 is about cognitive effort, mental and economic energy, and information entropy. We explain why people may only have three energy levels based on the empirical research (Yang, Braine, & O'Brien, 1998). Thus, from a microeconomic perspective, a consumer can be characterized by three indifference curves and three only.

Section 11.7   organizes an artificial debate about the "twenty questions" game between a great physicist, John Wheeler, and a great computer scientist, Allen Newell. Professor Wheeler claims that it is necessary for quantum physicists to play the twenty questions game against nature. Professor Newell claims that we cannot beat nature by playing the twenty questions game. We will explain why each side only represents half of the science behind the question and why both halves are necessary. As mentioned in Chapter 1, this book continues the research on the mind and the economy, following Professor Wheeler's advice. We do not intend to beat nature, the mind, or the market;

however, we aim at having a better understanding of them, even with limited observational powers.

Section 11.8 summarizes the logical map used thus far to move toward a quantum theoretic and quantum field theoretic model, effectively integrating economics and cognitive science. Normative theories used in economics and higher cognitive research are gauge theories, which are used as standards to normally gauge economic and sub-economic worlds. These normative theories possess global symmetries based on their standard meta-properties. Normative gauge theories are paired with null observations and are useful in defining stationary states.

Empirical research involves non-null observations. As argued in Chapter 1 (theoretical) and Chapter 10 (empirical), global symmetries of normative gauge theories are spontaneously broken once empirical research makes non-null observations. At this stage, cognitive psychology is committed to investigate commonly shared cognitive routines, which cost minimal cognitive efforts or mental energy. Thus, cognitive routines (as well as ordinary rationality to be discussed in Chapter 15) are the basis states, which are also called physical vacuums. The disadvantages of the trivial symmetry breaking approach used in current psychological theories and behavioral economic theories will be compared with the advantages of the spontaneous symmetry breaking approach applied in the present book.

Notice that cognitive routines (or ordinary rationality) are mostly degenerate states (i.e., a kind of states that are generally tied with other states and hard to isolate given the limited number of eigenvalues) with nonzero but constant vacuum expected values. Hence they are analogous to the *Higgs field* in theoretical physics. When more challenging tasks are performed, which demand more effort and higher mental energy, the corresponding mental states can be characterized by accelerated states. Given the Higgs fields as basis fields, we may assign (by testing) the relative difficulty (i.e., mass) of an accelerated state. This is what is meant by the modified version of the Higgs mechanism (in analogy to its counterpart in physics). Because only the Yes/No type of experiments are involved, the projection on each eigendimension is a wave function, whose amplitudes are characterized by complex numbers. It is important to consider the exponential form of any complex number, as it allows us to introduce the notion of gauge transformation ($\Phi \rightarrow \Phi' = e^{i\gamma}\Phi$) and phase space. The application of the quantum field theoretic approach in economics and cognitive modeling will be the contents of Volume III.

0.3 *The Detailed Outline of Volume III: Quantum Field Theoretic Models at the Sub-economic and Market Levels*

Mainzer (2005) pointed out, "In the 19th century, predecessors of modern mathematical economics propagated the use of the mathematical methods of physics in economics. Actually, much of their vocabulary was borrowed from mechanics and thermodynamics, for instance, equilibrium, balance, stability, elasticity, expansion, inflation, contraction, flow, force, pressure, resistance, reaction, movement, friction and so on." This tradition has been proven to be quite productive in the development of neoclassical economics. The present approach follows this tradition but extends beyond the classical mechanics. Even though the analogical models presented in this book are qualitative, they have the potential for quantitative outputs. Chapter 12 introduces a quantum chromodynamics model (QCD) of sub-economic analysis. Chapter 13 introduces a quantum electrodynamics model (QED) of market. Chapter 14 further applies ideas of quantum field theory (QFT) to integrate economics and cognitive science.

Chapter 15   begins by reviewing various notions of rationality in economics and in cognitive science; then proposes four principles (selectivity, subjective certainty, null action, and sunk cost) for the idea of ordinary rationality, which will have applications in both cognitive science and economics.

Chapter 16   discusses the notion of the potential market, which is a sensitive issue following the financial crisis in 2008 and during periods of economic downturn. There are different kinds of competing rationalities affecting the potential market; they follow the law of superposition but not the addition law. The principle of slave (a physics principle associated with laser light theory) is applied to explain why ordinary men determine whether a potential market can become real.

Chapter 17   explains the experimental nature of the human economy. The following principle is proposed: The more aware people are of the experimental nature of the economy, the smoother the development of that economy. The economy of China is analyzed as an example of this. In each chapter of Volume III, not only will real world problems be discussed, but we will also address deeper, more theoretical issues, ultimately proposing principle-based modeling methods. There is a logical relation from Chapter 15 to Chapter 17; ordinary rationality is the key to understanding the potential market, which in turn determines the experimental nature of economy. The ideas of Higgs field and Higgs mechanism, virtual process, and effective field theory are applied in Chapters 15, 16, and 17, respectively.

Chapter 18   provides open topics for modeling of mesoscopic economics. The modeling methods are modified from atomic physics, string/M-theory, and Randall-Sundrum model in theoretical physics. It first explains what we mean by modeling of economic analysis at the mesoscopic level. Second, it introduces five mesoeconomic factors and their intrinsic properties such as spin. Third, it introduces several quantum numbers such as rationality level and mental energy bundle, and provides a modified vector model. Fourth, it establishes the strong-weak duality between economic factors and the socio factor by modifying the ideas from string theory. Fifth, it studies a simplified case concerning the interaction of domestic economy, social stress, and international relation. This simplified case is modeled in steps by consulting the insights from the Randall-Sundrum model and the ekpyrotic approach in cosmology. The outline of Chapter 18 is relatively long in the present chapter, as the topics are open but deserve more explanations.

Chapter 12   A QCD Theoretic Model of Sub-economic Analysis

Section 12.1   first revisits the well-known invisible hand conjecture by Smith and provides a critical review of von Mises (1949) regarding human action. We analyze the relation between the "individual impulse" (von Mises, 1949) and "self-regard" (Smith). We argue that by its very nature, the individual impulse is twofold: the achieving motivator leads to self-regard (termed Impulse 1) and the fear-of-failure motivator leads to the awareness of other's regard in the market process (termed Impulse 2). There is a key difference between the present approach and the Austrian school of economic thought. In the latter, awareness of other's interests is the second nature of an individual (not the first); while in the former, awareness of other's interests is the other side of an individual's first, intrinsic nature because it is based on the fear-of-failure motivator. Then, it briefly introduces three intrinsic characteristics (i.e., id, self, and superego) of the individual impulse (based on Freud and others).

Section 12.2   briefly introduces the basic concepts and ideas of the QCD. The fundamental idea here is to ontologically refer Impulse 1 as a mental up-quark and Impulse 2 as a mental down-quark. Three intrinsic characteristics are described, referred to as different color charges. Here, we distinguish the intrinsic impulse from the demand for commodities; they are closely related but belong to different levels. The notion of demand is analogous to the electron in the QED models (see next chapter). Mental quarks carry integer color charges but fractional demand (electric) charges. The bounded states of mental quarks move from the sub-economic level to the economic level. An economic proton (E-proton) consists of two mental up-quarks and one mental down-quark; it carries one unit demand (electron) charge. An economic neutron (E-neutron) consists of two mental down-quarks and one mental up-quark; it is demand-neutral. Here, we will introduce a specific kind of symmetry, isospin, of E-protons and E-neutrons. The economic nucleus (E-nucleus) refers to a bounded state of E-protons and E-neutrons; the number of E-protons included determines the degree of demand charge of an E-nucleus. The next section answers the question of "How is a bounded state possible?"

Section 12.3   treats consciousness as a strong sub-economic force and treats each conscious state as an economic gluon (E-gluon). Note that this idea was first prepared in Chapter 3. Being conscious of a number of E-quarks is the way to bound them together. In analogy to the strong interactions described in QCD, asymptotic freedom maintains validity in conscious fields at the deep sub-economic level. Section 12.4 develops a minimum QCD theoretic model at the sub-economic level and shows how it holds a symmetry characterized by SU(3) in group theory. The analogies used in this chapter are shown in the table below.

Table for Chapter 12:
A QCD theoretic model at the sub-economic level

Implicit intentional marketing charge in fraction	Virtual goods spun (1/2) by two opposite intentional directions		Quarks in QCD — 3 generations and 6 flavors			3 color charges & their anti-charges in QCD	3 types of Freudian personality as sub-economic color charges
Two impulse types	Spun up ↑	Spun down ↓	1st gen	2nd gen	3rd gen		
+2/3 — Impulse 1 by achieve motivator	Wanted ↑	Anti-wanting →	Up quark	Charming quark	Top quark	Red/anti-red Green/anti-green Blue/anti-blue	Id Self Superego (with their antitypes)
-1/3 — Impulse 2 by fear of failure motivator	Given ↑	Anti-giving →	Down quark	Strange quark	Bottom quark		
Quarks have fraction e-charges — Impulse 2 may lead to other-regards	Sensitive to the awareness of possible costs as virtual price		Low	Middle	High	8 mixed color charges of gluons	8 types of sub-economic consciousness
	3 levels of subjectivity weight (see above)						

Isospin of bound states: proton (uud) and neutron (ddu)

Bounded by consciousness as sub-economic gluons

Sub-economic proton, write p:
[Impulse 1][Impulse 1][Impulse 2]
Virtual marketing charge +1

Sub-economic neutron, write n:
[Impulse 2][Impulse 2][Impulse 1]
Virtual marketing charge neutral

Chapter 13   A QED Theoretic Model of Market Dynamics

Section 13.1 formulates the key market elements. A demand (analogous to electron e⁻) and a supply (analogous to positron e⁺) have two components: a trader (whose intention is responsible for the market charge to buy or to sell) and a property (responsible for being spun). The notion of market action will be introduced. Accelerations of demand and supply are sensitive to price (analogous to a photon). The taxonomy is shown in the table below.

Table for Chapter 13:
A QED theoretic model at the elementary economic/market level

Marketing charge	Potential participant	Action charged	Property/Goods/service		Market particles	Analogy to QED	Electric charge
			Spun up ↑	Spun down ↓			
m^-	Potential buyer	Buying	Bought ↑	Anti-bought ↓	Demand	Electron	e^-
m^+	Potential seller	Selling	Sold ↑	Anti-sold ↓	Supply	Positron	e^+
Neutral			(Sensitive to price)		Price	Photon	Neutral

A market element can be real, written as [action, property], or virtual, written as [intention, property]. Each market element is attached with a market field. The taxonomy given above is purely syntactic, in analogy to electric field. By the symmetry requirement of logic charge for a system (see Section 0.2 and Chapter 2 in this volume), the corresponding semantic component needs to be characterized in order to explain the dynamic of the system. Here, what has been missing in the picture is the economic counterpart of the magnetic field. To be consistent with the current account in theoretical physics, without ontologically admitting the so-called magnetic charge, we need to provide an account of how the market field can yield to and interact with a cognitive field (in analogy to the magnetic field). This is a sensitive issue because in the present framework, money should be characterized by the market-cognitive wave (or price as its quanta).

Let us consider a virtual demand as an example without loss of generality (as the discussion about supply is similar.) A virtual market element can be created and annihilated. During the lifespan of a virtual market element, there is a spinning process that goes back and forth between "to buy" and "not-to-buy." To modify the concept by Penrose (2004), this process can be characterized as an internal "zigzag" process, which, in turn, produces the internal market "current". This process is consistent with our common experience (recall what we often do when thinking of buying something.) The market current can be treated as the source to produce the corresponding cognitive field with two cognitive poles (in analogy to magnetic field with the magnetic poles N and S). One may consider this cognitive field as a rationality field, which involves reasoning with two logic poles (true or false) or involves decision making with preferential poles (prefer one choice to another). It is not hard to imagine that the interaction between the market current and the corresponding cognitive poles is sensitive to price in monetary terms.

Similar discussions concerning a pair of demand and supply or concerning many market elements, which can be characterized by the "in-between" zigzag processes, will also be provided in Chapter 13. In these cases, the notion of market potential is introduced to produce market current. The corresponding mathematical model (in terms of spinor field and Dirac equation) will be described and discussed qualitatively in Chapter 14, Volume III.

Section 13.2 briefly introduces the conjecture by Wilczek (2008), "Maybe, in our quest for unification, we haven't been ambitious enough. The soul of our unification of different charges is this:

electron ↔ quark
photon ↔ gluon

This still leaves the building blocks of the world divided into two separate classes. Can we go further? Can we do this?

electron ↔ quark
↕   ↕
photon ↔ gluon

Let's try." Consider the taxonomies given in two tables above (Chapter 12 and Section 13.1), the same issue is addressed here, shown below, but in the analogous context of the interactions between sub-economic and market levels.

demand ↔ impulse
↕   ↕
price ↔ consciousness

Section 13.3 briefly introduces the core concepts and ideas of quantum electrodynamics. Special attention is paid to ideas such as "off shell mass," negative energies, virtual particles, and virtual process. These ideas will then be applied to the modeling of sub-economic analysis. We introduce the notion of virtual action and virtual price in terms of market processes (when impulse energy is low). The virtual process is an intermediate process (called j-process) and costs mental energy, which is allowed to be nonconservative (Pais, 1986) due to the uncertainty principle (Randall, 2005).

Chapter 14 Quantum Field Theoretic Interactions

In Chapters 12 and 13, mental components are structured into economic elements (e.g., demand and supply) which are no longer point-like elements, but field-like instead. Section 14.1 selectively applies quantum field theoretic language and concepts to characterize interactions of economic elements at sub-economic and market levels.

Section 14.2 introduces the creation and annihilation operators for supply and demand, which are sensitive to monetary terms such as virtual and solid prices (economic photons). Mental components are not only responsible for the market charges of economic elements, but they also cause the corresponding market magnetic moment. The concepts of an economic vacuum and vacuum fluctuation are discussed, which permit virtual economic excitations and processes.

Section 14.3 briefly introduces Pauli matrices, the Dirac equation, the Dirac sea, and antiparticles. In an economic sense, the concept of self-control is a robust consumer phenomenon. The notion of "economic meson" refers to the bound state of an impulse and its anti-impulse.

Section 14.4 is about interactions. A number of sample collisions are discussed; examples are given in the table below:

Table for Chapter 14

Sample collisions in economics	Analogy to QFT
price + economic proton $\rightarrow$ economic proton + demand	$\gamma + p \rightarrow p + e$
price $\rightarrow$ demand + supply	$\gamma \rightarrow e^- + e^+$
economic neutron + policy $\rightarrow$ economic proton + demand	$n + W \rightarrow p + e + v$

Section 14.5 briefly introduces the Feynman diagram method and uses it to characterize the creation, annihilation, and collisions of economic elements. Section 14.6 addresses two open issues: (1) How to replace classical margin analysis by Lagrange formalism and functional analysis and (2) How to apply the minimum action principle in economic analysis.

Chapter 15   Ordinary Rationality and Higgs Field

Section 15.1 makes historical remarks on the development of rationality theories. Since the time of Plato and

Aristotle and for about two thousand years after that, the primary focus of rationality was on reasoning. Since the 1940s, the focus has switched to decision making. We will explain why and how this transition occurred.

Section 15.2 discusses why the notion of the ordinary man is difficult to define. It is a sensitive issue in the psychology of law, particularly in the jury selection process.

Section 15.3 reviews various current theories of rationality in cognitive science and economics. Further discussions on economic rationality and personified markets are included. The notion of the bounded rationality umbrella is revisited with the following approaches: (i) Simon's ideas (such as the model of business men, the architecture of the decision process within an organization, and that people pay more attention to outcomes rather than to choices). (ii) Kahneman and Tversky's idea about cognitive norms, and Gegerenzer's claim on the effects of environment and experience. (iii) Economic irrationalities by Amartya Sen. Lastly, (iv) Rationality 101 by Johnson-Laird.

Section 15.4 proposes four principles in theorizing ordinary rationality as its theoretical cornerstones.

The *principle of high selectivity* states that because there are limited resources, ordinary people are highly selective in formulating their choices. This does not necessarily imply that ordinary people are bounded by the information; rather, given this information overloading time, it means ordinary people are very intelligent with how they distribute their energy, where to pay their attention, about what business they have to take care of, and what role they should play in public affairs. At these points, ordinary people are not passively bounded, but rather they are intelligently selective. Ordinary people know what to do as well as what not to do. They know what to accept, as well as what not to accept, based on the common sense.

The principle of subjective certainty is based on Wittgenstein's idea that although the world is full of uncertainties, ordinary people have established a great deal of subjective certainties. People take actions only when it is really necessary. Wittgenstein studied various kinds of uncertainties, such as language games, in most of his writings. He is called the leading philosopher of skepticism in the 20th century. However, Wittgenstein entitled his later book: *On Certainty*. He claims that doubting everything is not a doubt. One can only doubt what one believes in. In everyday life and in common economic life, ordinary people do most things routinely based on subjective certainties they have established from their experience or based on their norms. This is an inertial system of their everyday life. For example, a student got up in the morning and was walking on the way to class. There was always a possible uncertainty for the class to be canceled, but this student went to the class meeting anyway. At this point, this student was doing what people ordinarily do: they are simply acting rather than taking an action, which are two different things. Without subjective certainties, it would make ordinary people feel nervous in daily life, which is ordinarily treated as abnormal or irrational.

The *principle of taking null action* states that people often take null actions in making decisions. Taking the null action is an action. If we denote the routine acting by an empty set ø, taking null action

least action principle

should be denoted by {ø}. The routine acting costs a minimum level of mental energy and cognitive effort. In taking a null action, ordinary people intend to keep the mental energy and cognitive effort at minimal levels. The two might not be distinguishable at the behavioral level, but can be different at the cognitive level. In modern decision theory and in economics, taking a possible action means to give up an alternative action as the opportunity cost. Ordinary people take non-null actions only when it is really necessary. The examples of taking a null action, such as preferring not to prefer, halting from buying, or abstaining from voting, are too many and too common. It is a special kind of decision making, which is so ordinary that it seems overlooked by current decision theories and from economic modeling. In the real world, people often take many null actions before taking a non-null action. In the business world, a manager is less likely to report null actions taken than to report non-null actions, as these two kinds of decisions are usually not evaluated equally. A leader who takes too many non-null actions may be seen as lack of experience or vision by ordinary people. A person who takes non-null actions too often would make ordinary folks nervous.

The *principle of sunk cost* claims that the sunk cost is routinely taken into account when people ordinarily make decisions. Textbooks in economics always teach us that economics is about efficiency: given the scarce resources, it studies the most efficient allocation. The margin analysis is concerned only with the present or near future: if we invest one more unit resource, what would be the margin cost and the margin gain. It is not about what happened before, so that sunk cost is irrelevant. However, the sunk cost is an intrinsic property of ordinary men; it partly represents who they are. An ordinary investor who keeps holding a stock when its price is going down might due to the sunk cost in his or her account. To ordinary people, and even to an organization, sunk cost may mean many things, which are not necessarily monetary. Sunk costs could include personal loyalty, private mental investments, the expectations from friends and relatives, social stress, etc. All of these sunk costs, in turn, may well affect the economic development and organizational decision or reform because any policy has to go through ordinary people, who are rational in common sense. By the standard model of particle physics, all the gauge particles are massless and they can be assigned their masses (could be massless) only by interacting with Higgs particles, which will be briefly mentioned below and explained in detail in Volume III.

In addition, people ordinarily only consider three choices or fewer (reduced to simple judgment if only one choice is available), and they are ordinarily capable of making three and only three levels of effort. Thus, a consumer shall be characterized by three and only three indifference curves. If more than three levels are offered, without special training and extra efforts, ordinary people will routinely cluster them into three groups. At this point, understanding ordinary rationality is a key to understanding the potential market.

Similar to the case of cognitive routines mentioned in Chapter 11, ordinary rational states can be best characterized by the idea of the Higgs field in modern theoretical physics. Economic rationality characterizes stationary states, while ordinary rationality is related to those basis states containing minimal energy levels. Similar to the Higgs field, ordinary rationality has the following properties. First, it is everywhere so it can be seen as a field. Second, it serves as a scalar field because the effect of any policy or the price of a commodity is determined by the ordinary people at the bottom line. Third, ordinary rational states can hardly be isolated from and are always tied with other states, so ordinary rationality is a degenerated state. Fourth, ordinary rationality is an inertial system in everyday and economic life. It can be characterized in terms of a vacuum. Finally, ordinary rationality keeps or intends to keep not only the economic cost, but also the cost of mental energy and cognitive effort at the minimal level. This effort is not zero, the corresponding vacuum can be seen as with constant nonzero vacuum expected value. To give an intuitive illustration about the Higgs mechanism, we will borrow the metaphor of "moving the arms in the water" by Randall (2005). In set theory, we have $\{\varnothing\} =_{df} 1$, where $\varnothing$ represents the empty set. We use this presentation to illustrate how the modified economic version of Higgs mechanism works, particularly, in how people ordinarily deal with "economic Goldstone elements" in order to assign economic weights (e.g., values or masses) to commodities, services, and policies.

Neoclassical economics is centered on the concepts of economic rationality and general equilibrium; it should be treated as a set of gauge theories and gauge concepts with global symmetries based on null observations. These gauge theories define the economic and sub-economic stationary states. When cognitive models and empirical research with non-null observations are taken into account, the global symmetries of these gauge theories are spontaneously breaking.

Chapter 16   Potential Market and Virtual Contributions

Section 16.1 begins with D. North's talk at Beijing Forum (2004), entitled "Economics and Cognitive Science." Mental states, such as belief, are closely related to the economy. This has become more significant since the 2008 financial crisis when confidence in the economy became a crucial issue. All monetary and fiscal policies worldwide are about potential markets, but a satisfactory theoretical account for the potential market has been lacking.

Section 16.2 argues that sunk costs matter to ordinary rational men, while the margin analysis used in current economics excludes sunk costs. Sunk costs are a testing bed to study individual differences in rational mental states toward the potential market.

Section 16.3 shows that competing rationalities follow the law of superposition but not the law of addition which makes the potentiality of the economy spin, thereby causing quantum fluctuations. Some quantum theoretic methods are applied here from modeling perspectives (e.g., complex numbers and Feynman path analysis).

Section 16.4 discusses a special but common phenomenon called the "standing-by participant" effect. It reflects taking serious null actions on the market. A standing-by participant can be an ordinary investor or consumer, or even some big "hot money" holder, who is an active observer and may take non-null actions at any given time. Here, I will discuss what is meant by the virtual price analogous to a virtual photon. As an example, let us consider the stock market. For a given trading day, a stock had an opening price as its initial state. Suppose a trade happened at a higher price one hour later as its final state. Assume that during this hour, an intermediate price was on the screen, but no trade happened on this price. During this hour, if we treat this intermediate price as static, then we have to admit that the clock is moving. Now let us assume it happens in a four-dimensional space-time, in which the intermediate price was in motion all the time during that hour, as in this framework the time is a fixed dimension. Since this intermediate price is neither in the initial state nor in the final state, it is a virtual by definition; as we analyzed, this intermediate price should be treated as a moving virtual price. During this process, assume some investor intended to buy the stock or to sell the stock at this intermediate price, we can say the moving virtual price created a pair of virtual demand and supply, in analogy to a moving virtual photon creating a pair, a virtual electron and a virtual positron.

Section 16.5 applies the principle of slave to the rationality analysis. Because ordinary rationality is the most stable type of rationality among competing rationalities, it possesses the strongest capacity to react to policy intentions. Eventually, it dominates the direction of the superposition of possibilities within a potential market.

Virtual quantum contributions (Randall, 2005) and virtual processes may have an effect on solid interaction. It should be noted that this view has been taken seriously in theoretical physics (Pais, 1986) but has been purposefully neglected by current economic theories. We will provide some remarks on how to take virtual processes into the realm of economic modeling.

Chapter 17   The Experimental Nature of Economy and Effective
              Field Theory

As we have claimed in this volume, human economy is, by nature, experimental. This should not be confused with current experimental economics. Section 17.1 starts to review the long standing controversies between Keynesian and the free-market schools of economic thought. We claim that all the economic theories looking into the future can only be hypothetical and need to be empirically examined. The economic practice is the final judge.

Section 17.2   examines being an economist as a profession; it has a special privilege associated with policy making. We push the question to the extreme. With the damage as high as $700 billion, economic advisers or financial leaders have only two choices: either confess guilty or acknowledge that the economy is an experiment. The saying, "the model is good but the underlying assumptions or pre-conditions did not meet", will be questioned.

Section 17.3   reviews the economic development of several selected countries. The principle postulated here states the following: the better the understanding of the experimental nature of human economy, the healthier and faster a nation can develop its economy. We will briefly introduce the recent development of QFT: effective field theory, which provides useful tools for modeling from a policy-making perspective. In QFT, renormalization is use perturbation method to eliminate the infinities. The insight of renormalization will be applied in modeling the process of economic policies. However, economic policy does not solve all the potential social problems. In the standard model of particle physics, the renormalization is unable to deal with the infinity caused by gravity, which is spin 2. In economic mechanics, this means economic policies is not enough to deal with social pressures, particularly during the economic downtown. This issue will be addressed in Chapter 18 (see its outline below.)

Section 17.4 studies virtual measurement and testing underlying the surface of an economy. Given the experimental nature of human economy, the participants of economy (which can be individuals or any organizations) must be treated as designing thier own experiments. They are motivated to revise their experimental designs from time to time, based on their observations, self-testing, self-measurement, and self-judgment. These virtual processes are not directly measurable from the surface of economy. In physics, the current real measurement is at the level of 10^{-19} but the theoretical modeling has reached the level of 10^{-36}. The processes between the two levels are treated as virtual. In analogy, we have to model virtual phenomenon underlying economy and possible virtual phenomenon that could happen toward future economy. A great deal of empirical investigations is well documented in the literature, but the modeling methods need to be advanced. This section is devoted to initiate possible advancements by formulating a QFT approach.

Chapter 18   Open Topics for Modeling Mesoscopic Economics

This concluding chapter describes a set of ideas to deal with some traditional topics concerning current macroeconomics, political economics, and international relations. The strategy is to study intrinsic properties of macroeconomic factors by applying modeling methods borrowed from atomic physics. The idea behind this strategic treatment is that in forward observation (see Chapters 1 and 2) of these factors, the degree of disturbance is high and thus the world is small.

Section 18.1   addresses three issues from modeling perspectives. First, there is an assumption underlying current macroeconomics: the economy is, in general, going up with various kinds of business circles. I will characterize this phenomenon by describing a thought-experiment in analogy to the well-known Frank-Hertz experiment (1941) in atomic physics.

Second, the current modeling methods used in macroeconomics are based on the idea of "large number". This is the reason why statistical means and summations can be applied in formulations (e.g., the GDP formula). This is similar to the case in macroscopic physics. Here, macro-phenomenon means post-decoherence states. In studying micro-phenomena, due to the intrinsic properties, such as spin of particles (also economic elements), the coherence of waves must be taken into account. In macro-analysis, when a great number of particles are considered collectively within a system, particle interactions are assumed to cancel out with each other. This is called the decoherence process, reflecting the average effect of interactions (Wang, 2010). Thus, in macro-analysis, the intrinsic properties of particles (and economic elements) are neglected.

Third, there is another level of analysis (and modeling) between micro-analysis and macro-analysis, which can be called the mesoscopic analysis. Decoherence is a complex micro-process. Mesoscopic analysis studies a system with a large number of elements while the effects of coherence still need to be taken into account. By the diagonal law of scientific observation introduced in this book (see Section 0.1 and Chapter 1), the forward observation into future economy is with a high degree of disturbance. Hence, it is zooming into a micro-world, in which any economic factors must be characterized by a probability wave from a quantum theoretic viewpoint. Thus, the coherence of probability waves needs to be taken into account. In this book, the economic analysis and modeling at the mesoscopic level is called "mesoeconomic analysis". We expect that modeling at the mesoeconomic level may provide explanations about business-circles at macroeconomic level.

Section 18.2 introduces five kinds of mesoeconomic factors and briefly characterizes their corresponding intrinsic properties such as spin. The first kind of mesoeconomic factor refers to the pure economic activities. Economics studies possible allocations of scarce resources. Economic theories assume the concept of efficiency as their main theoretical concern. It is useful to refer to efficiency as the "economic change", which can be positive or negative. Pure economic activities include those activities directly involved in productivity and market action. In analogy, pure economic factors represent the nature of economy, which can be compared to fermions in physics. Similar to the spin of most fermions, pure economic factors are considered to have a spin of ½. Intuitively, one can count some resource completing

one possible allocation as a one-dimensional rotation
of 180 degrees, assuming 360 degrees as the base.

Some other kinds of mesoeconomic factors may affect the
efficiency of economy; hence they also carry economic charge.
The second kind of mesoeconomic factor is of economic policy and
administration. This is a kind of force that can affect the growth
or decay of the economy and regulate economic activities. It can
encourage or discourage certain economic activities. It can be seen
as spinning twice as fast as pure economic activities. We consider
it as having a spin of 1. It is analogous to the weak force in physics,
which only works over a short distance (or short run in economy).
From particle viewpoint, policy and administration is analogous to
the family of W-particles. We know that they are heavy in economics
as well as in physics. The third mesoeconomic factor is money. In a
modern economy, for a given product, money is charged and paid;
for a certain productivity, both investment and benefit are described
in terms of money. Hence, when pure economic activity completes
a rotation of 180 degrees, money needs to rotate 360 degrees. In this
sense, money has a spin of 1. As argued in other chapters, money is
analogous to the electromagnetic force or photon in physics. From
this particle viewpoint, it is price (analogous to photons, see Chapter
13) that has a spin of 1.

The fourth mesoeconomic factor is social tension, which
obviously may affect economic efficiency and hence carries
economic charge. In Chapter 6, economic gravity (or graviton) is
characterized by possible Pareto improvements everywhere. We
know that economic developments and economic policies may
cause wealth redistribution all the time. This may well serve as the
source of social-economic tension, which in turn may seriously
affect the efficiency of the economy. This is clearly the case seen
during the worldwide financial crisis and economic downturn.

In economics, the notion of Pareto efficiency is not concerned with fairness. Now let us imagine a two dimensional picture. The horizontal dimension is purely economic with rare resource and allocation as two ends. It carries economic charge of efficiency. The vertical dimension is purely political with individuals and administrations with policy at two ends. It carries political charge of fairness, which can also be either positive or negative. This picture can be used to explain that when the pure economic factor rotates 180 degrees and when the policy as well as money factors rotate 360 degrees, the social gravity factor has to rotate 720 degrees in order to achieve social symmetry, which is necessary to keep the conservation of society. In other words, an economic change of large scale could cause roughly four times the social tension and political effort. For illustrating rotation and symmetry, the example using pokers by Hawking (1988/1996) and the example using books by Penrose (2004) are good references.

The fifth kind of mesoeconomic factor is tradition and habit. In mesoeconomic analysis, it serves as various inertial systems, reflecting what people are used to doing and the way they are used to conducting economic activities. It can be characterized by ordinary rationality (see the outline of Chapter 15) and is affected by the principle of sunk cost. Similar to inertial systems in physics, the factor of tradition is of spin 0. This factor can hardly be neglected in economic modeling as we all know how strong it can be. In physics, inertial systems of spin 0 often break beautiful symmetries (T.D. Lee, 1988). I will provide a detailed discussion about what this means in mesoeconomic analysis in Volume III.

In general, it is easier to sense the causal relations between pure economic factors and other factors carrying economic charge than to understand the casual relations between physical fermions and bosons. We know that any economic activity has a social impact and vice versa. These bi-directional impacts are dichotic at each direction. This may be related to the idea of super-symmetry and Fermi transformation in superstring theory, which seems more natural in social science than in physics; this issue will be discussed further in the book.

Section 18.3   briefly introduces the notions of several quantum numbers in atomic physics and then applies their insights to initiate a model for mesoeconomic analysis. An economic factor state can be characterized by three quantum numbers: rationality, factor spin, and cognitive direction. Compared to atomic physics, rationality is characterized in terms of the main quantum number, denoted by "n", which accounts for the energy levels. Factor spin is characterized by the angular quantum number; it should consist of orbital momentum and spin momentum. Here we will only be concerned with the angular momentum of factor spin, which is denoted by "l". The corresponding cognitive directions are characterized by the magnetic quantum numbers (each with two projections), denoted by "m" (and m_s). It provides the idea about the economic version of a vector model. We will also introduce the notion of rational charge and make an estimation about what we call the quantum economic constant. These topics will be briefly explained below.

In this volume, we have introduced three "charges": logic charge (syntactic vs. semantic), market charge (sell vs. buy), and economic charge (efficiency with positive or else negative sign). The fourth charge we need to introduce is called the *rationality charge*, which can have either a positive sign (being rational) or a negative sign (being irrational). The first quantum number needed, called major quantum number, to determine an economic factor state is the level of rationality, denoted by n, which reflects the level of economic energy. Similar to the concept of leveled energy bundle in atomic physics, rationality is discrete but not continuous with gauge theoretic viewpoint. The reason for this is two-fold, which is explained in the following.

The mesoeconomic factors described involve plans, strategies, and many possible economic activities and paths that carry rationality charge. Thus, these factors can only be gauged by different gauge theories of rationality, such as economic rationality, bounded rationality, or ordinary rationality proposed in this book. These rationalities are principled with internal structures, which are embodied in mesoeconomic factors and, in turn, can be used to characterize the possible orbits of a factor. The possible orbits are in levels, which determine the levels of rationality because in order to reach a given level of rationality, demand a certain level of mental energy and cognitive effort in action. A given amount of energy and effort are often not enough to achieve this next level of rationality.

On the other hand, we need to take into account a higher order cognitive process embodied in economic factors. At this point, rationality charges are carried by reasoning, decision making, and game theoretic behaviors. For example, in deductive reasoning, it is performed in steps. To complete a reasoning step, it requires a certain amount of mental energy and cognitive effort. Here, it does not count if one only gets "half way" through. The internal structure of a reasoning problem characterizes the orbit of mental activity at this point. For inductive reasoning, one jumps up to a hypothesis from a number of facts established. In the case of decision making, preference is a binary relation, meaning the choices are to be compared pair by pair, and likewise for action profiles in game theoretic interactions. A great deal of empirical evidence supporting this view is well documented in the literature (e.g., Yang, Braine, & O'Brien, 1998; Yang & Johnson-Laird, 2000). In this sense, rationality is gauged in discrete accounts.

The angular quantum number in physics consists of orbital angular momentum and spin angular momentum. By this time, the present author lacks clear insight about how to characterize the orbital angular momentum for an economic factor; thus we can only speak of spin angular momentum, which is denoted by l. As a quasi-vector model, each spin angular momentum l can yield a number $(2l+1)$ of polarization directions, called the magnetic quantum number, calculated by the formula $(m = -l, -l+1, \ldots, l-1, l)$. In mesoeconomic analysis, a factor spin may also polarize different cognitive directions. The spin quantum numbers and the corresponding magnetic quantum numbers for the five mesoeconomic factors are summarized briefly in the table below.

Table for Chapter 18

Mesoeconomic Factors	Spin Quantum Number	Magnetic Quantum Number	Cognitive Directions (projections)	Analogy to Physics
Tradition	0	{Ø}	1	Inertial/Vacuum
Pure-economic	1/2	-1/2, 1/2	4	Electron
Policy/Regulation	1	-1, 0, 1	6	W particles
Money	1	-1, Ø, 1	5	Photon
Economic Gravity	2	-2,-1, Ø, 1, 2	9	Graviton

In physics, photons and gravitons are purely relativistic particles; they have a magnetic number of 0 in the mathematical representation, and have no corresponding physical phenomenon.

Thus, in the table above, notation calls for the empty set Ø, instead of 0, to denote that it has no corresponding economic phenomenon. Also, graviton is not included in the context of standard model of particle physics; it is included in the table above for comparison purpose, and will be discussed in the next section.

Section 18.4 discusses two dualities by consulting with the idea of strong-weak duality in string theory. One is the duality between market charge and cognitive charge, and another is what can be called the diagonal duality between the pure economic factor and the social factor.

In Chapter 13, the notions of demand and supply are defined in terms of intention and commodity (or service). By this definition, the intention component carries a market charge (to buy or to sell). During the life span of this demand, for a given price, the market current yields a cognitive field of thinking. It goes back and forth between buying and the control of buying. This cognitive process can be polarized with respect to making the decision. This can be compared with the classical description of the electromagnetic fields. The motion of electric charge yields the current. This then causes the magnetic field which is responsible for polarization to have pole moments. In string theory, it emits both electric charge and magnetic charge. By Dirac's principle, the multiplication of electric charge and magnetic charge must be a constant. In other words, it satisfies a kind of strong-weak duality: the stronger the electric charge, the weaker the magnetic charge, and vice versa. From this point of view, we may admit both market charge and cognitive charge in our modeling, which also satisfies the strong-weak duality of a similar kind: the stronger the market charge of a demand, the weaker its cognitive charge. If one has stronger intention to buy, he thinks less; if his intention of buying

$$M = C = L$$

is weaker, he needs to think more. One of the strengths of the string theoretic language is of being sensitive to different dualities, which might be overlooked otherwise. These dualities disclose important meta-properties of a system. The following is another kind of duality which is also generated from common sense.

Traditionally, quantum field theory treats particles as point-like entities and pre-assumes that they interact at a space point, which is zero dimensional. By this view, it allows the change of position for a particle to approach zero, which by the uncertainty principle implies that its momentum approaches infinity. This is one of the reasons why the current standard model does not deal with the graviton, as there is no perturbation method available to renormalize the infinity caused by a spin 2 particle. In our case, one may imagine that if the social stress focuses on one point in the economy, it would carry some infinite power that is more than enough to break the economy at any point. At this point, string theory admits the notion of a string with an extended length. It is defined as one dimensional, such that it can spread the interaction strength. This is more similar to the interaction between economy and social stress. Notice that in physics, the length of a string is very tiny, while by the orthogonal principle (see Chapter 1), in economics, the length of a "string" with respect to an economic factor can be large with possible complex vibrations.

The string theoretic concepts also bring some new degrees of freedom in characterizing a string. Its tension and its strength, which are inversely proportional, the greater the tension of a string, the weaker its strength is for interaction (because it is harder to pluck.) Now let us characterize the economic factor and the social factor (here it refers to the economic gravity, see Chapter 6) in terms of their tension and strength. For the economic factor, the inversely proportional relation is that the poorer the economic situation (i.e., the stronger the tension), the harder it is to simulate the economic activities (i.e., the weaker the strength). For the social factor, the inversely proportional relation is that the smaller the degree of satisfaction about the economic situation (i.e., the weaker the tension), the higher the degree of the social stress (i.e., the stronger the strength). Thus, the interactive relation between the economic factor and the social factor can be shown as in the picture below:

Picture 1 for Chapter 18

Social factor string

	Strength	Stress
	←	←
II		I
S/S	S/W

Economic Hardness ↑   ↓ Activeness
Factor String Tension ↑   ↓ Strength

	S/W	W/W
III		IV
	→	→
Tension	Satisfaction

(Note: the inverse arrows stand for inverse proportional)

The picture above illustrates a causal relation between the economic string and social string, which has two possible cases. To illustrate, in the first case, start by assuming that the economic situation is bad, and hence the social satisfaction is low. Accordingly, the strength of economic activity is weak and the social stress is strong. Thus, in the picture, Quadrant I and Quadrant III show the diagonal strong-weak duality between economic string and the social string. It also shows diagonal isospins at Quadrant II and Quadrant IV. In the second case, one may assume the economic situation is good, and by the same logic, we have a mirror symmetry picture of the above. In string theoretic terms, we may call the duality within a picture as the quasi-S-duality and the duality between two mirror-pictures as the quasi-T-duality (target space duality).

Section 18.5   addresses issues concerned with the global economy and international relations. From the last section, we can infer that during a domestic economic downturn, the internal social stress within a country becomes high. The same can be said about more than one country when the economic downturn is global. Consequently, to the common observation, the international conflicts increase in general. This section models a simplified case by consulting with the string/M-theory, the Randall-Sundrum model, and the so-called ekpyrotic scenario in cosmology. The model can be outlined in the following seven steps:

Step 1   is to adopt a three-dimensional space. In microeconomics, a large number of n goods or bundles, they can be clustered in terms of inference curves, each of which represents a certain level of utility. Empirical research (Yang, Braine, & O'Brien, 1998; and see Chapter 11, Volume II) demonstrated that ordinary people are routinely capable of perceiving three levels of differences and three levels only. This makes sense to convert an n-dimensional analysis into a three-dimensional framework, in which each individual participant can be characterized by a vector.

Step 2   is to introduce 3D-branes (one can imagine them in terms of membranes) into the model. From the string theoretic viewpoint, a 3D-brane is a three-dimensional entity that can be extended in a three-dimensional space with any shape. By the convention in string theory, here the discussion is based on the 3+1 dimensional space-time, but only the number of space dimensions is identified for introducing a brane.

Step 3   is to treat economic factors, including economic policy and monetary factors as open strings. These factors are standard gauge economic factors. Accordingly, we call the corresponding open strings gauge strings. The social factor is treated as closed strings, analogous to the graviton as we described in Chapter 6.

Step 4   is to build two (or more) standard 3-branes in the three-dimensional space (or 3+1 space-time), call them Economic-Brane X and Economic-Brane Y. Each economic brane stands for the economy of a nation. An open string (representing economic factors) has two endpoints, each must be attached to an economic brane. There are four possible ways at this point. If both ends of an open economic string are attached to the same brane, it is called a domestic economic string, written as (X, X) or (Y, Y). If one end is attached to the first economic brane and the other end is attached to the second economic brane, it is called an export string, written as (X, Y) or (Y,

X). As a convention, for example, (X, Y) means an export from the country X to the country Y.

Step 5   is to add an extra space dimension to build a five-dimensional space-time, called a bulk. Let us call it the international socio-economic bulk. The extra dimension can be seen as the dimension of value. Different nations may share some values and may well hold some different values. Because the monetary factor is confined to the 3+1 branes, certain value conflicts in international affair cannot be solved by money. This is also probably one of the reasons why this extra dimension is often overlooked from pure economic perspectives. In Chapters 3–5, we characterize money as the light of economy; thus, the fifth dimension is monetarily "dark". The nationally oriented economic 3D-branes are inserted into this international bulk. The social factor, analogous to the graviton, is characterized by closed strings, which are not confined to a brane but are free to travel in branes and in the bulk.

Step 6   introduces the certain dynamic structure into the setup outlined in Steps 1–5. In the current step, we need to modify the Randall-Suntrum model (write RS1 for short) to serve our terms. The original RS1 model considers a pair of branes, one visible brane and one hidden brane, in a five-dimensional space-time. The visible brane is called the Weakbrane which holds gauge interactions. The hidden brane is called the Gravity-brane. The two branes are located at the boundaries of the fifth dimension. One can imagine the two branes to be face to face in a warped space-time and they follow a graviton probability function. Now, in our model, let us first consider two visible branes, X and Y, where each stands for the economy of a nation in the five-dimensional global bulk. The insight here is borrowed from Randall's (2005) ideas about sequestering and localizing particles, in particular, the gravity.

The RS1 model is not a string/M-theory approach, but let us borrow the string theoretic language here. As explained in Step 4, we have four types of open economic strings: (X, X), (Y, Y), (X, Y), and (Y, X). Now, assume the economic situation turns down in an economic brane. As we analyzed in Section 18.4, the strength of economic strings becomes weaker but the strength of the social stress factor (gravity) becomes stronger. Notice that in the action function of RS1 model, there are three negative cosmological constants (thus the anti-de Sitter space applies), one for each of the two branes and one for the bulk. Here the negative cosmological constant can be understood as the intrinsic rationality (collectively it may involve cultural, ideological, and other factors) for an economy to bounce back. So we may call it a socio-economic constant. Thus, on the one hand, to prevent the internal social gravity from stressing the economy, the local negative socio-economic constant with its repulsive gravity effect acts to "squeeze" the social stress potential to leave the economic brane. Here I modified the descriptions of RS1 model by R. Maartens (2006).

On the other hand, assume two economic branes are both experiencing economic downturn. The international relation between the two is under global social-political stress. For example, right after the 2007 global financial crisis, the whole world was sharing a common stress. But by Randall (2005), particles can be sequestered and localized. That is the rationale for the RS1 model to have the hidden gravity-brane. Similarly, we have observed that soon after sharing the global economic stress, it is politically sequestered into the nationalized stresses, due to the weakened strengths of (X, Y) and (Y, X) type economic strings. At this stage, the negative global socio-economic constant with its repulsive stress effect acts to squeeze the sequestered global socio-economic stress to each corresponding local economic brane. At this point, for each economic brane, the internal social stress has been squeezed outward and the external political stress has been squeezed inward. Consequently, the same two-sided squeezing process yields a localized hidden socio-economic stress brane X' to the economic brane X and a Y' to Y.

Step 7   is to consider two new combined branes, XX' and YY', each carrying strong international stress. As the gravity type stress, the two new branes may well be highly charged to "attract" each other, which can be modeled as the cause of what we used to call the potential international conflict. Here there are two models in recent theoretical physics that may provide insights for our further modeling efforts. One is the Goldberger-Wise solution, and the other is the ekpyrotic universe approach.

In Randall's words (2005), the Goldberger-Wise "*solution relied on two competing effects, one that favors widely separated brane and another that favors nearby brane. The result is a stable compromise position. The combination of the two counteracting effects leads naturally to a two-brane model in which the two branes are a moderate distance apart.*" This would be ideal in international relations between two or more countries, but we need a mechanism in our framework.

For the ekpyrotic universe approach, let me quote from McMahon (2009), "*In this model, we are imagining a universe which has always existed, but which goes through a cyclic pattern. This pattern begins with an initial state characterized by the boundary branes living in a flat, empty, and cold state. They are located at the boundaries of the fifth dimension and are parallel. In the ekpyrotic scenario, the branes are moving, so they move toward one another and collide. The collision of the branes, a process called ekpyrosis in the literature, is seen as the "big bang". The energy from the collision creates the matter in the brane. After collision, the branes move off apart from one another, and cool down. Eventually they return to the cold, empty, flat initial state, and the process begins all over again."* This approach seems to force us to allow nuclear war in solving international conflicts, which is obviously not attractive to Mankind.

The model outlined from Steps 1–7 above can be partly pictured below.

Picture 2 for Chapter 18

(X, X) strings (domestic on X)

Economic gauge D3-brane X
the socio-economic constant Λ_x

Virtual socio-economic gravity brane X*

(X, Y) strings
(Export from X to Y)

A five-dimensional bulk
the international bulk constant Λ:
$+\Lambda$: attractive to gravity
$-\Lambda$: repulsive to gravity

(Y, X) strings
(Export from Y to X)

Virtual socio-economic gravity brane Y*

the socio-economic constant Λ_y
Economic gauge D3-brane Y

(Y, Y) strings (domestic on Y)

My proposal is to assign the rationality charge to the socio-economic constant, which can be positive or negative. In other words, the socio-economic constant should be treated as a rational operator instead of a constant. Mankind supposes to be capable of switching the sign of socio-economic charge rationally. Nature does not need to switch the sign of cosmological constants because it does not run experiments, it does not make mistakes, and it has no need to account for any cost. Nevertheless, our civilization does and must, although sometimes we switch the rationality sign to a wrong direction.

Section 18.6 is a philosophical discussion about possible connections between the framework of economic mechanics and the Planck's constant, which is arguably the most basic conceptual cornerstone in quantum theory. Toward the end of this book, it is an open topic that I still unable to provide either quantitative or qualitative initiatives. Nevertheless, there should be no reasonable excuse to escape from speculating the possibilities on this issue.

Planck's constant, denoted by h, is a very small bundle of energy in particle physics (one can imagine it at the level of 10^{-34}). Historically, Planck's constant was introduced qualitatively as a theoretical rule in characterizing the discreteness of energy. It was then fixed its quantitative measure after many experiments and calculation. Each step took years and cost a great deal of efforts by physicists such as Planck who made persistent effort while other had given up. The book will briefly review several examples involving Planck constant, such as radiation of blackbody, required energy level and orbits of the electron in the atomic structure, uncertainty principle (i.e., $\Delta x \Delta \rho \approx h$ or $\Delta t \Delta \varepsilon \approx h$). Notice that in most of the equations in quantum theory, Planck constant often occurs with imaginary i in characterizing quantum theoretic equations such as wave equations.

I will provide some insights about what the economic or cognitive counterpart of Plank's constant would look like. First, as I argued in the outline of 18.3, rationality is discrete, which implies that mental energy and cognitive effort should be counted in terms of discrete bundles.

Second, by the orthogonal law and the diagonal law (see Chapter 1), the constant should be some gauge within a range that can be characterized in the reciprocal direction (i.e., inverse proportional) of Planck's constant h. In other words, it must be something that is complex enough to raise the high disturbance in our forward observation into the future economy or inward observation into higher cognition. It is surely an open and challenging topic to figure out what this "$1/h$" can be referred to in economics, theoretically first and empirically next. The speculation is that $1/h$ would indicate the mesoscopic level for conducting economic analysis.

Third, given the current stage of theorizing, we had better to strategically treat the counterpart of Planck's constant in the present framework as a running constant across different phenomenon and, more realistically, to treat it as a jumping constant from one topic to another topic. It would serve as a working hypothesis for further theoretical effort to establish equations needed.

Fourth, there are many kinds of uncertainties studied in economics and cognitive science. By the similar research strategy, we need to formulate different versions of the uncertainty principle based on a theoretical constant. And, finally, by working through the above steps it would provide us more insights about how to empirically estimate the quantity of these constants.

The insight from atomic physics to mesoeconomic analysis is rich. The extended discussions and more technical introductions will be given later in the book (Volume III).

Chapter 1

Principles Concerning the Directedness of Observation

Perhaps you have heard the witticism: "What is mind? No matter. What is matter? Never mind." Though of course open to debate, the general thrust of this quip seems to be that the mental is nonphysical (or at least not profitably studied as if it were physical) and that the study of the physical should be ignored by those studying the mind. Regardless of whether or not the aphorism was originally intended to convey this, there can be no denying that this rather dark interpretation is today found congenial by many. And at any rate, even those who are passionately seeking to reduce the mind to a physical machine, so that eventually psychology collapses into physics, must admit that, at present, such reductionism remains, at best, a dream.

Yet both mind and matter have been and continue to be studied scientifically, of course; and while cognitive science is a much younger field than physics (and its partner, mathematics), it is well known that traditional psychophysics and neoclassical economics (e.g., Marshall, 1926) were in point of fact influenced heavily by classical Newtonian mechanics and its conceptual framework. On the other hand, it must be conceded that higher-order cognitive research (such as the study of reasoning and decision making and behavioral game theory) has been lagging behind lower-order cognitive research, such as the study of perception, sensation, and action. The reason for this lag, put simply, is that when it comes to higher-order cognition, which is, by definition, that part of the human being addressed by economics, classical mechanics is the wrong branch of physics to leverage. In this chapter, we start to present an alternative approach, which goes beyond classical mechanics to quantum mechanics. The global financial crisis of 2008 is an urgent call to economists, one that specifically demands a deeper understanding of the mental processes, consideration of which gave rise to the formalisms at the heart of neoclassical economics. What is the theoretical foundation for our new line of modeling? A set of ten principles are given for this new approach; four in this chapter, six in the next.

1.1 *Directions of Observation*

Unlike matter, a great part of the human mind is unobservable; nonetheless, human beings have never stopped trying to observe the mental world. Researchers want to scientifically investigate, and rigorously model, how the mind works (including, but not limited to, mental equipment, mental representations, and mental processes). Yet we must be wary of the fact that most theories about the mind are hypothetical and need to be empirically justified; the hypotheses in these theories can only be represented in a statistical language. By its very nature, therefore, cognitive science is an empirical science. A well-trained professional in this domain would never say, "I have proved something." Proofs are notions used in analytical methods, which are at the heart of mathematics and logic. A well-trained professional is suitably circumspect and would therefore say that the empirical evidence "tends to confirm" the predictions made by the model, and thus, the theory is rendered more plausible.

Under these constraints, an important question arises: as well-trained cognitive scientists, what method do we have at our disposal that allows us to study the mental world as rigorously as physicists do when modeling the physical world? In other words, what can cognitive modeling share with theoretical physics? One thing it can share can be described in terms of *observation*. Here, we propose a useful distinction as our first working conceptualization without further argument for it—the scientific observations can be classified in two ways: we have *outward* observation of physical world, and we have *inward* observations of the mental world. Accordingly, we assume this as our first working hypothesis:

Principle 1.1 (orthogonal observational directions): Scientific observations are directional. The inward observation of the mental world and the outward observation of the physical world are in opposite observational directions.

In the next chapter, we claim that human economic activity itself is experimental *per se* and that it also involves directional observations. The study based on historical data should be treated as involving *backward* observations, which has a low degree of disturbance. The study of future economic development and Smith's "invisible hand" driving the market can be treated as involving *forward* observations, which, in general, have a relatively higher degree of disturbance. Of course, inward observations in macroeconomics, as well as in microeconomics, may be necessary when mental states (such as *confidence* or *belief* or *mental preference*) are to be modeled as endogenous variables.

Scientific observations are performed through carefully designed experiments. This is the second thing cognitive science shares with physics. Similar to experimental designs in physics (and to other natural sciences), good experimental designs in psychology require various kinds of experimental controls, including testing materials, procedures, and participants. Critics sometimes blame psychologists for putting too many experimental controls in experiments. This sort of attitude constitutes unfair treatment of the empirical research of mind. Indeed, physicists would acknowledge that in their experiments, experimental control is what it's all about. So it seems unfair to question the controls, including positive reinforcements, used in psychological experimentation. We will pay more attention to this issue in later chapters, when empirical researches are introduced. For example, a good experimental design in quantum physics aims to have the right experimental setup, with high-energy and well-prepared materials, in order to accelerate the targeted particle. A good experimental design in psychology of reasoning aims to use well-worded testing items with clear inference structures, as stimuli to be entangled with the targeted cognitive capacity; it is assumed that when the target capacity is accelerated, the original mental, phenomenological world collapses.

Another fact, which we assume as a presupposition, is that there is always certain *friction* against the body with respect to mental processes. We can't stop people from getting tired when exerting sustained cognitive effort for the fact that people have limited mental energy for effective thinking. That is also usually why an experimental session lasts no more than one mere hour.

1.2 Types of Experimentation

Given the limitations of experimental methodologies, both in cognitive and physics research, there are generally certain degrees of *disturbance* in observations. This notion will be explained in more detail when analyzing specific experimental tasks in Chapters 10 and 11. Often, in books written to introduce nonclassical physics such as quantum theory or theories of relativity to nonexperts, some cartoons or personified examples are given in order to show how the mind would think and perceive physical phenomenon beyond our everyday intuition (e.g., Hawking, 1996, 2001). For example, when a father goes out to do yard work, his two boys are peacefully watching TV; when he returns to the house, the boys are still watching TV peacefully. What happens between his observations is that the boys have a fight while he works in the yard. This ministory can be used as an analogy to explain the concept of *quantum fluctuation* (Greene, 1999). Similarly, some different kinds of quantum fluctuations happen when inward observations are performed. For example, when it takes longer than a minute for a participant to complete an experimental trial, say solving an SAT item, there is generally a five-second mental daydreaming break or confusion to disturb observation when the latency data is being collected. In some type of experiments, the disturbance is small and can be ignored; in certain types of experiments, it matters. Taking this into account and following the great insight of Dirac (1930/1958), we have:

Principle 1.2 (disturbance): The higher the degree of disturbance in the experiment, the smaller the world can be observed.

What kind of experiment has a low degree of disturbance, and what kind of experiment has a high degree of disturbance? The principle of disturbance actually provides a way of distinguishing two very general types of experiments. One can be characterized as the *smooth* type of experiment with a low degree of disturbance; the other can be characterized as the Yes/No type of experiment (von Neumann, 1955; Penrose, 2004), with a high degree of disturbance.

The more formal introduction and mathematical definition of Yes/No type experiments will be given in later chapters. Here, we only provide an intuitive way to understand the levels of scientific observation. As an example, imagine a picture of an iceberg (in a rather different sense from what Freud used to analyze subconsciousness). This image allows us to distinguish three levels of research. For the first level, one is on the iceberg; this level enables the researcher to make a map of the parts of the iceberg above the water line. This can be compared with behavioral research in psychology as well as in economics. For the second level, assume that a boat equipped with advanced measurement technologies is near the iceberg; it allows the possibility of simulations, in order to estimate the approximation of the landform of the iceberg under the water. This can be compared with cognitive computational modeling research in cognitive science. Both the first and the second levels of observation have a relatively low degree of disturbance and are accordingly treated as "smooth" experiments. For the third level, suppose the boat is in a certain distance from the iceberg; it only allows us to see the top of the iceberg. It is this third level of observation that carries a high degree of disturbance and shall be treated as the Yes/No type of experiment; it is this type of experimentation that this book focuses on. Why is the third level research as important as the first two levels? At this moment, one may recall the movie *Titanic* as an illustration.

1.3 *The Orthogonal Law and the Diagonal Law*

The distinction between smooth vs. Yes/No experiments should be general enough to cross observations of the physical world, observations of the mental world, and even that of the economic world. Given this distinction, we are now ready to turn to some key ideas; the analogies given in Table 1 might seem somewhat counterintuitive for now, but they will prove to be very useful later on.

Table 1

Experimental World Type of Experiment		Macro-world Smooth Experiment	Direction of Observation	Micro-world Yes/No Experiment	Direction of Observation
Fields & Domains	Physics	Newtonian mechanics	Outward	Quantum mechanics	Outward
	Psychology Cognitive Science	Psychophysics Lower cognition (perception, sensation)	Inward	Mental mechanics Higher cognition (reasoning, decision making, game theory)	Inward
	Economics	Neoclassical economics Margin analysis	Backward	New economic mechanics	Forward
Type of task (inward) Measurement in time		Computer simulation, priming task Millisecond matters		Verbal task, etc. Second or minute	
Degree of disturbance Operational law		Low disturbance Additive states		High disturbance Superpositional states	
Character of statistics		Smooth learning curve		Probability wave function, amplitude	
Math description		Continuous functions, differentiable		Delta-function, singularity	
Logic foundation		Classical standard logic		Quantum logic	
Mathematical tools		Mathematical analysis, differential equations, real analysis, etc.		Functional analysis, Hilbert space, measurement theory, Feynman diagram, Dirac *bra-ket* formal system, etc.	
Field of numbers		Real numbers (without observer)		Complex numbers (with observer i)	

To follow the map presented in Table 1, one first needs to make an ontological commitment to the so-called experimental world. Penrose proposed a three-world picture (1997/2000) consisting of physical world, mental world, and "Platonic" world. Here, the Platonic world is also called the *analytical world* (i.e., the mathematical or logical world). Penrose is a very capable mathematician, who has a deep understanding of quantum physics; he did an excellent job in developing mathematical tools for theoretical physics (2004). However, he would have had an even greater contribution if he had taken an experiment-oriented approach to the study of the mental world (though he wrote beautifully about scientific study of mind (1989, 1994, and 1997). A similar thing can be said of Chomsky, who is probably the greatest cognitive linguist. The question we are interested here is in what sense, from the modeling perspective, can the study of the mental world, and the study of physical world, share parts of the Platonic world (i.e., share the right branches of mathematics and logic). We propose that this challenge can be better addressed if the experimental world is admitted as the fourth world, which consists of *experimental things* according to Whitehead (1920/2000, 1927–1928/1978). This idea can be represented by the chart below.

Chart 1

Physical world
                    → Experimental world → Analytical world
Mental world

Then we can introduce the following principle:

Principle 1.3   (orthogonal):   Experiments   in   the   study   of higher-order cognition and experiments in the study of quantum physics are in the spectrum of the same type of Yes/No experimentation, and share a great deal of the same kind of mathematical analyses.

Accordingly, in economics, we have,

Principle 1.4   (the Economy Principle): Human economy is, by nature, experimental. It involves backward and forward observations. Forward observation is of the Yes/No type experimentation.

The orthogonal principle only spells out half (which is mostly relevant to the present book) of what can be called *the diagonal law*. To spell it out fully, let us start by zooming in on Chart 1, and by doing so, we obtain:

Chart 2

Case 1 Classical mechanics

Case 2 Quantum mechanics   (1, 3) Smooth Experiment → Continuous Function

Case 3 Lower cognition   (2, 4) Yes/No Experiment → Delta-Function

Case 4 Higher cognition

From Table 1, we can give a few cases, as shown below:

Case 1   Consider the classic Newtonian mechanics that uses outward observation of the physical world. Here, the target moves slow and has a larger size; the degree of disturbance in the experiment is low, and it can be described by a smooth curve. It is about the macro-world for observation by Principle 2.

Case 2   Consider the traditional psychophysics that uses inward observation of the mental world. It mostly studies sub-domains of lower cognition, such as vision, audition, sensation, perception, human-computer interaction, etc. The experiments mostly use computerized simulation and priming tasks, in which each single trial is simple when millisecond matters when measuring; thus its degree of disturbance is relatively low. Accordingly, in an hour-long experimental session, a large number of trials can be tested. Given the high density of trials, the distribution of raw data can be approximated as a smooth learning curve, and characterized as a differentiable function.

Thus, from the experimental perspective, the above tradition of psychophysics is about the observational macro-world, and it shares a great deal of mathematical elements with classical Newtonian mechanics. Here, the term *lower cognition* has a new meaning: viz., cognition having a lower degree of disturbance when observed. This book is not about the orthogonal cases that are 1 and 2; this book is about the following orthogonal pair of cases found below:

Case 3   Consider quantum mechanics, which uses the outward observation of the physical world. It is well known that target physical particles, which are accelerating, are very small in size and move fast. By Dirac (1930/2004), the degree of disturbance in quantum experimentations is high; thus such experimentation is about the microworld by Principle 2.

Case 4   Consider the new mental mechanics, which this book is devoted to. This mechanics applies inward observations to the mental world. It investigates higher-order cognitive tasks, including human reasoning, decision making, and game theoretic interactions. These sub-domains are major contents of the following chapters, and will be introduced respectively in an integrated way, and their experimental characters are spelled out repeatedly as needed in different contexts. Below are several characteristics of higher-order inward observation:

First, the experimental items used in these domains are designed with formal structures, reflecting the normative theories, which are more complex than the priming trials used in lower-order cognition experiments. Second, the predictions are made based on the corresponding psychological models, which are compatible with normative theories. Third, the experimental items are verbal tasks, given in natural language(s). Fourth, it used to be measured in seconds or minutes (contrary to the case of priming tasks, where milliseconds matter). And finally, the number of trials (experimental items) is relatively small in an hour-long session—much smaller than that of lower-order cognitive experiments that is. These characteristics allow various kinds of thinking fluctuations during the information-processing period. In this sense, the experiment is with a high degree of disturbance; thus, by Principle 2, the corresponding observational world is micro, meaning the degree of what is observable is low. (As a general, extreme case, one can imagine the logical reasoning items found in standardized tests, such as the GRE or SAT, as implications.)

Because the mental representations and mental processes in higher-order cognitive tasks are not directly observable, the tests of this kind are typical Yes/No experiments. In most reasoning experiments, the so-called evaluation tasks are performed. Given a set of premises, the participant is asked to mark "YES" or "NO" for a putative conclusion provided. In the experiments of decision making and behavioral game theory, the preference order is a binary relation. In preferring A to B, it means that one is making A yes and B no. Even multiple choice problems are, by nature, often times, Yes/No type problems.

Given the initial descriptions of Cases 3 and 4, we should get some basic insight into the reason why new mental mechanics can share the Yes/No type of experimentation with quantum mechanics—and we will. Consequently, we later demonstrate that mental mechanics shares a great deal of its formal and mathematical tools with quantum mechanics.

In a more abstract sense, the orthogonal law reflects a *symmetric* relation, in terms of the characteristics of observational targets between inward and outward observations across physical and mental worlds (as can be seen in Table 2).

Table 2

	Experimental Characteristics	
Disturbance / Observation	Low Macro-world	High Micro-world
Outward	Slow / Large	Fast / Small
Inward	Fast / Simple	Slow / Complex

The phenomenon represented in Table 2 deserves some more general discussion. As T. D. Lee (Nobel Laureate in Physics, 1957) said at one point, "At this stage, it may be worthwhile to pause and indulge in some abstract thinking" (1988).

1.4 *Non-observables and Symmetries*

What abstract thinking should we carry out here? As we mentioned earlier, both physics and cognitive science/psychology are, by nature, empirical sciences. They both study observables as well as non-observables; the border between observables and non-observables seems to continuously change as experimental technologies advance. Consider Principle 1, with some revisions of Table 2, the symmetric relation can be seen as plotted in Figure 1 and Figure 2 below:

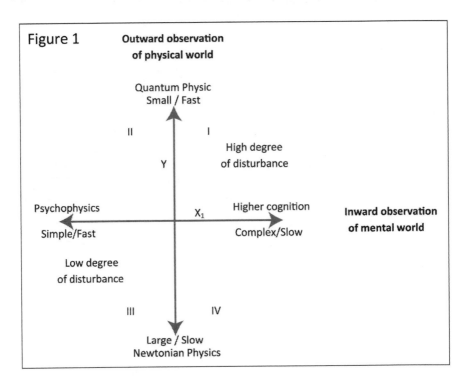

Figure 1

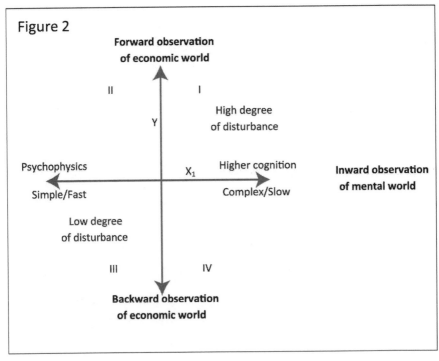

Figure 2

This is a special case of symmetry, which can be called cross-domain *second-order symmetry*. T. D. Lee (1988) once gave some great insight: *"Indeed, all symmetries are based on the assumption that it is impossible to observe certain basic quantities, which we shall call 'non-observables,'"* and *"non-observables imply symmetry."* Using logic, this idea can be represented as a universally quantified statement with the individual variable ranging over the empty domain, which is the case for any predicates. This also serves as one of the key ideas in the next chapter, which is used to understand the relation between the so-called invisible hand and the ideal of a free market in economics.

Chapter 2

Principles Concerned with New Economic Mechanics

2.1 *Gauge Theory and Symmetries*

To continue the discussion about symmetry, it will be useful to borrow some concepts from quantum field theory. We will do so in Volume II and heavily in Volume III. Higher-order cognition and current economic theories are naturally related neighboring disciplines due to the fact that they share two standard normative theories, namely, modern axiomatic decision theory and game theory. What has been overlooked in current economics is logic, which is the third standard normative theory for higher-order cognitive research. We will argue it is important to study the reasoning process underlying decision making (see Chapter 9, Volume II). These normative theories are crucial because they serve as the gauge theories to guide us to gauge the targeted mental capacities and economic behaviors. Indeed, these gauge theories not only help us to identify the targets we are interested in, but also help us to observe the phenomenon (e.g., in designing of experimental items). This is a concern particularly sensitive to observations with high degree of disturbance, such as outward observation to particle behavior, inward observation to higher-order cognitive tasks, and forward observation into future economy.

These gauge theories have a special kind of internal symmetry. A standard logic system needs to satisfy two meta-properties— soundness and completeness (see Chapter 7, Volume II)—which can be represented as follows: for any given set of premises Γ and a conclusion A, we have

$$\Gamma \vdash A, \text{ if and only if, } \Gamma \vDash A \qquad (2.1.1)$$

The left side denotes a proof (i.e., infer A from the premise set Γ.) Here, proof is a purely syntactic concept in standard logic (see Chapter 7, Volume II). The right side says that it is a valid argument form. The validity is a purely semantic concept in logic. Similarly, in decision theory, we have the meta-property called representational theorem (see Chapter 8, Volume II) given as follows: for any given choices C_i and C_j, we have

$$C_i \succ C_j \text{ if and only if } ME(C_i) > ME(C_j), \qquad (2.1.2)$$

which reads as that C_i is preferred to C_j if, and only if, the mathematical expectation of C_i is greater than the mathematical expectation of C_j. Similar to the case in (2.1.1), the notion of preference is purely a syntactic concept in decision theory, and the notion of mathematical expectation is a pure semantic concept in the so-called number theoretic model (i.e., utility semantics) to decision theory. Notice that the meta-properties represented in (2.1.1) and (2.1.2) are given by universally quantified statements, so they must indicate a kind of global symmetry. Also, keep in mind that when we talk about observation in cognitive science or in economics from an experimental perspective, it always involves two components: the item and the participant, or say, the target of an observation and the observer.

From (2.1.1) and (2.1.2), we can see internal structures of a special kind of symmetry. For a logical item, if we know it is semantically valid, we then also know it is syntactically provable and vice versa. Thus, for the any given logical form, its semantic side and syntactic side are symmetric. For a decision theoretic item, representation theorem says that for any pair of choices, if we know its syntactic preference, then we also know which choice has a higher mathematical expectation than another and vice versa. Borrowing the idea of isospin between proton and neutron in particle physics, we can see analogically a kind of isospin between the syntactic side and the semantic side of a logic item or a decision item. Several points are worth mentioning here. First, modern logic is probably the best studied formalism, which made clear the distinction between formal syntax and formal semantics, which followed with the formulations of modern decision theories (Savage, 1956; Jeffrey, 1965). Without the hint of this leading formalism, we might miss the idea of isospin in decision theory, in game theory, and in economics.

Why is the idea of isospin concerned here? One of the reasons is that it is related to the definitions of rationality and irrationality. For example, By Sen (1985/2002), if one prefers C_i to C_j, but in actuality, $ME(C_i)$ is less than $ME(C_j)$, it is called the correspondence irrationality. By the same token, if $ME(C_i)$ is greater than $ME(C_j)$, but one does not prefer C_i to C_j, it is called reflection irrationality. In the next section, the notion of economic rationality will be introduced based on the decision theoretic structure, where we will see similar internal symmetry given the internal structure within the definition of economic rationality.

The internal isospin of an item can be seen as a special kind of global symmetry. To follow Zee (1986/1999), this kind of global symmetry means once the proof is treated as syntactic and the validity treated as semantic, everyone has to follow. This seems a bit strange to be called global symmetry; however, we will explain why it is very useful shortly. It is useful to introduce another kind of global symmetry concerning observers. The notion of global symmetry can be best compared with special theory of relativity. In Minkowski space-time, every point represents a permissible observer (Naber, 2006). Given the speed of light as the invariant, every permissible observer observes the same speed of light under Lorentz transformation. This is called global Lorentz symmetry. We will talk about this in Chapter 5, where the speed of money will be treated as an invariant.

When individual observers are allowed to have different views or stances toward "the event," which may be anything, they are required to mean the "the same event." For the same event, individuals can have different views, but their views need to be communicative in order to connect one observer to another. This is characterized by local cured frames in general theory of relativity assuming the curved space-time. In this case, we say that they can be connected and covariate. This is called local symmetry in physics. In Chapter 6, we will model the notion of Pareto efficiency (which allows individual differences) of economics in terms of geodesics, where the general theory of relativity will be applied.

Still, why do symmetries matter? As emphasized in Chapter 1, physics, economics, and cognitive science are empirical scientific domains. They always involve experimentation and observation. An observation always involves two components: an observer as the subject and the target as the object. In the special theory of relativity, it involves the speed of light as the target and observers characterized by inertial systems. In quantum theory, if one wants to study a physical state φ, written $|\varphi\rangle$, you run an experiment Φ to observe it, written $\langle\Phi|$, which can also be seen as the arrival final state after experimentation; the inner product $\langle \Phi \mid \varphi \rangle$ is called Dirac's *bra-ket* formalism of quantum theory (see the outline for Section 8.3 in Chapter 0). The quantum theoretic meaning of that $\langle \Phi \mid \varphi \rangle$ is called the amplitude, which is characterized by a complex number, $a+ib$. To illustrate, consider the example of testing an electron. Because it can spin up or spin down, we need to test it at least twice and return the real term a and the imaginative term ib. The resulting amplitude could be a zero by the superposition law. In $a+ib$, "i" may be read as information obtained from observation or simply read as the observer "I" (Ni, 2004). In cognitive science, an observation involves the experimental item and the participant. In economics, for example, the demand can be formulated by a pair of the intention that is responsible for market charge and the targeted commodity that is responsible for being spun (see Chapter 0 in this volume and Chapter 13 of Volume III).

To follow the earlier discussions, we may identify three kinds of symmetries, in which we are interested. Write [α, ψ] as a kind of observation, where α is the target for the observation. Here ψ can be given in three cases. Case 1: ψ is the set of all the permissible observers. This is similar to the case in special theory of relativity; it is a kind of global symmetry, call it Symmetry 1. Case 2: ψ is a set of functions, each of which is associated with an observer, and these functions covariate. This is a kind of local symmetry, call it Symmetry 2. Case 3: ψ is an empty set of observers, but it seems strange to have $\psi=\varnothing$, where $\varnothing$ stands for the set of null observers. This is the situation similar to treating the internal isospin as a kind of global symmetry, which holds the null observation with every observer. So it would be better characterized by $\psi=\{\varnothing\}$, where $\{\varnothing\}$ stands for the set of null observations of the observers. In predicate logic, this is exactly the case to say that a universally quantified statement is always true when the object domain is empty. Call it Symmetry 3 and name it *trivial global symmetry*.

Still, again, why do symmetries matter here? In this volume, we will deal with a number of fundamental concepts in economics including money, Pareto efficiency, and economic rationality. These three can be seen as gauge concepts in economics, each related to a kind of symmetry: money is related to Symmetry 1, a kind of nontrivial global symmetry (see Chapter 5). Pareto efficiency is related to symmetry 2, a kind of local symmetry. And economic rationality is related to Symmetry 3, a kind of trivial global symmetry.

Still, once again, why does it matter? As T. D. Lee pointed out (the original idea was by Emily Noether), symmetry implies conservation. The isospin of syntactic and semantic properties must imply the conservation of a special charge (which has been overlooked for long). We refer to this charge as "logic charge," which can be either the syntactic charge or the semantic charge in analogy to color charges of quarks in QCD. We say logic charge is conservative when the distinction of syntax and semantics is committed and the isospin of the two properties is universally quantified within a gauge theory or a gauge concept.

Given the conservation of logic charge for a gauge theory, we can further modify the notion of gauge field from the standard model in particle physics. The corresponding gauge particle is massless. In the present context, we call the corresponding gauge particle "rationality particle," which is difficulty-free or effort-free with the current null observation. Does this make useful sense? Yes. The internal structure represented by the isospin symmetry is necessary in order to gauge possible actions. The action description is used more often by particle physicists although it is equivalent to the differential description in physics. Many physicists regard the notion of action as more convenient to characterize interactions of particles. These physicists feel more convenient to use the term "interaction" instead of "force" (e.g., see Veltman, 2003). Gauge particles, though massless, function like mediums to make the interaction happen.

In economic mechanics, rationalities as gauge concepts (particles) serve as the medium to make interaction at the economic level, as well as the sub-economic level, possible. Economic gauge theories/concepts are also important for us, probably different from physics, to define stationary states with null observations from an experimental viewpoint. The internal structures help us to characterize actions during the interaction. In other words, internal structures carry the force to drive people to reason and to decide. One might ask about the role psychological theories (e.g., mental logic theory and mental models theory in psychology of reasoning as well as prospective theory in psychology of decision making) play in this picture. That role should never be overlooked. Indeed, as we will see, psychological theories will be responsible for checking out the coupling constants between a gauge field and other fields, by empirically determining, for instance, the degree of difficulty of a task. The previous paragraph and the present paragraph have gone beyond the scope I set up for Volume I of this book, as my intention is to make it conceptually self-contained, similar to the way I used to lecture in my classroom. I will make this up by introducing basic concepts and describing the ideas along this line in details in Volume II. For now, please allow me to just quote from Anthony Zee (1986/1999) as the concluding remark for this section:

> In action formulation, one takes a structural view, comparing different ways by which the particle could have gotten from here to there . . . . In discussing the concept of symmetry, I have taken great care to say that physical reality could appear different to different observers, but

that the structure of physical reality must be the same, the action principle allows us to make precise the phrase "structure of physical reality." (pp. 108–109)

The meaning of the action principle becomes clear by considering the prototypical process in which a particle starts at time t_A from point A and gets to point B at time t_B. In action formulation, we consider not only all possible paths between A and B, but also all possible ways in which the particle can travel the path. Thus, for a specific path, the particle may go slowly at first, speed up for a while, slow to a crawl, then speed up again. Physicists refer to each particular way of traveling the path in the allotted time as a "history." "A number, called the 'action,' is assigned to each possible history." (p106)

Now, I turn to the next section as we are ready to analyze one of the fundamental gauge concepts in economics, namely, economic rationality.

2.2 Economic Rational Man and the Market

The terms economic rationality and economic rational man (note the singular) are often used interchangeably in economic literatures. This is one of the conceptual cornerstones of the neoclassical economics. This concept has been frequently questioned by behavioral economics researchers since Simon (1947/1993, 1957) proposed the notion of bounded rationality. Bounded rationality aims particularly to characterize individual participants in a market; Simon calls these market participants businessmen (note the plural). However, most criticisms to economic rationality seem to have criticized the wrong target. I will explain why it is so.

The notion of rational man or economic rationality can be defined on the decision theoretic structure. The classic decision theoretic syntax has three layers. Layer 1 is a set of choices. Layer 2 is that each choice is followed by a set of possible outcomes. Layer 3 is that a possible outcome is characterized by two and only two properties: desirability and feasibility. The corresponding decision theoretic semantics, called the utility semantics, are then built from bottom up. The decision theoretic meaning of desirability is determined by a dollar value; the meaning of feasibility is characterized by a probability, which is determined by the normalized probability distribution on the set of possible outcomes associated with a given choice. The multiplication of the dollar value and the corresponding probability is a utility, which is the decision theoretic meaning of that outcome. Then the summation of the corresponding utilities of the set of possible outcomes returns the mathematical expectation of the given choice as its decision theoretic meaning. We will review this structure more formally in Chapter 8, Volume II.

Given the above decision theoretic structure, the notion of economic rationality or economic rational man can be defined accordingly. The economic rational man shall satisfy the following four requirements (Rubinstein, 1998):

Requirement 1: Full knowledge. This is a syntactic requirement, which assumes the rational man knows all the syntactic components of the decision problem, including all the choices, all the possible outcomes of a choice, and how to characterize an outcome by two properties such as desirability and feasibility.

Requirement 2: Full capacity. This is a semantic requirement, which assumes the rational man is capable of calculating the mathematical expectation for every choice from bottom up, based on a given utility function regardless of the design complexity. This should imply the capacity of optimization.

Requirement 3: Full scale preference order. This is a syntactic requirement. The preference order has to be established on, but not into, the set of choices. In other words, for any two choices, it has to prefer one to another and cannot prefer not to prefer. Given Requirement 2, the present requirement should be best understood as the meta-theoretic requirement. Namely, it should serve as part of the representational theorem bridging the decision theoretic syntax and the decision theoretic semantics as we explained in Section 2.1.

Requirement 4: Fully logical. It assumes indifference between logically equivalent descriptions. Economic rationalities are not affected by how the decision theoretic components are framed.

These four requirements received countless criticisms by treating the economic rational man as a possible individual market participant. Simon (1955, 1957) actually criticized Requirement 1 by proposing the notion of bounded rationality to characterize businessmen, which we noted were plural. There are also many well-documented debates and discussions about Requirement 2 that provide critical reviews concerning the limitation of individual capacities in performing the utility function. Different approaches, such as the causal decision theory (Joyce, 1999) and referential decision theory (Jeffrey, 1965/1990), were proposed toward the semantic components such as: value, probability, utility, and mathematical expectation. Requirement 3 received relatively less attention. We will introduce the notion of ordinary rationality and show that the decisions people often make is to prefer not to prefer. They often take a serious null action that is to not act. Kahneman, Slovic, and Tversky (1982) criticized Requirement 4; they proposed the prospect theory and studied framing effect. Let us leave the detailed discussion about these criticisms for later on. For now, the question is why the notion of economic rational man still standing firmly and what does it really stands for. Let us try to clarify this issue in the following three steps:

First, assume that the notion of an economic rational man is to characterize individual participants of the market. Then each participant, having the four capacities shown above, should be able to beat the market and get all the wealth. But such an individual participant has been so far invisible to us. How many such economic rational *man(s)* are on the market? If at least two existed, who would win?

Second, one might argue that in microeconomics, when the notion of the economic rational man is applied to model individual consumers, certain restrictions need to be added. It should be assumed that each individual consumer only deals with a finite number of goods. We will explain in the Section 2.4 that this restriction would break the mathematical foundation of consumer theory in which the existence theorem of a utility function depends on assuming a *countable infinite* set of goods. This is because the power set of this countable infinite set is equivalent to the set of real numbers; without the field of real numbers, it can neither define the continuous utility function nor a continuous preference order.

Third, theoretically, it is difficult to apply the notion of the economic rational man in characterizing any individual participant of the market. But there is one thing that fits this notion and may well satisfy the four requirements: *the market itself*. Now, we may rewrite the four requirements as four properties. Property 1 indicates that an ideal perfectly competitive market should be information-maximum. At this point, the market is the container of all the information as long as it exists. Property 2 is a good characterization of the power of the invisible hand. Property 3's emphasis is on the pricing function: any product has to be priced and, in turn, products can be compared by taking their prices into account. Property 4 says that the market cannot be fooled, cheated, or confused. However, the market has to be regulated and managed (e.g., bad financial items should not be repackaged to get a higher rating). Notice that the notion of the economic rational man is always expressed as a *man* (not *men*) which can only be used to characterize the personified market itself. Notice Simon used the term "businessmen" in framing his idea about bounded rationality.

Now, we have a clearer picture. The notion of the economic rationality is indeed a well-conceptualized structure. It consists of syntax (Property 1), semantics (Property 2), meta-property (Property 3), and inference rule (Property 4). The notion of *homo economicus* has confused people for quite a long time. It should not be misused in conceptualizing individual consumers. It is instead a platform for individual consumers to play on. It allows us to try to get more information, to observe how the invisible hand works, to take advantage of the pricing function, and to not violate regulations.

My approach here is to view the market as a huge economic laboratory. Economic rationality is the basic idea for experimental design. Accordingly, each individual market participant runs a particular experimental project. We have the following principle:

Principle 2.1: *Human economy, including markets, is itself experimental in nature. It involves observations at all levels. Each individual participant serves as the experimenter for his own experiment and as a subject for others' experiments. Economics should model this picture as a whole.*

From the analyses given in Section 2.1, the economic rationality shall be seen as a gauge theory. It has an internal structure showing the isospin between its syntactic requirement and its semantic requirement. It satisfies the internal global symmetry as promised by the representational theorem of decision theory. Traditionally, by the rational choice theory, the notion of economic rational man is characterized by the syntactic component "the agent prefers an action" and the semantic component "to maximize the personal profit." This individual structure must be consistently gauged by the internal isospin of the notion of economic rationality; thus, it follows a global symmetry.

One might wonder how the market is operated if it is characterized in terms of economic rationality but not of particular individual economically rational participants? Here is a rough idea on how it works. Economic rationality forms many kinds of gauge fields everywhere. It hires many invisible hands anywhere it goes. These invisible hands are with the titles called Economic Gauge Bosons (EGB). The EGBs act as mediums and are responsible for making interactions of economic elements happen. For instance, one kind of EGBs is what we used to call "price" (analogous to photon in physics, see Chapters 0 and 13). Another kind of EGBs is what we used to call "consciousness" (analogous to gluons in physics, see Chapters 0 and12). A third kind of EGBs is what we used to call "administrative power" or "government regulation" (analogous to vector Bosons), which is mostly responsible for economic element decay; for example, it can turn a fear-of-failure motivation to an achieve motivator (see Chapters 0, 14, and 16).

From the names of the listed EGBs above, one can imagine by the common sense that these EGBs themselves do not carry wealth (analogous to mass in physics); in other words, they are supposed to be wealth-less. However, on one hand, economics textbooks teach us that the market itself can yield wealth (e.g., by lowering the trading costs). On the other hand, some EGBs, such as the third kind above, do carry heavy wealth. How does that work? It has to be explained by a modified economic version of the so-called Higgs mechanism (in physics). These stories will be modeled and explained in certain details in Volume III. In the next section, we will only discuss the invisible hand in an abstract sense, assuming we know little about it.

2.3 *Invisibles and Observations in Economics*

Ever since Adam Smith initially mentioned about it, the concept of the *invisible hand* has long been a well-documented and powerful term in economics. However, in recent decades, the notion of the *invisible hand* has been a mysterious and controversial topic. The theory runs similar to a story: Individual productivity is motivated to serve the self-interest. Collectively as an economy, the individual productivities will achieve some unexpected results, which can be beneficial to the socioeconomic welfares. This dynamic process is driven by an undefined force called the invisible hand. This invisible hand is directional, and it should help in achieving the so-called Pareto efficiency for a perfectly competitive market.

The following case in a reasoning experiment (Yang, Braine, & O'Brien, 1998) may be similar to the case of the invisible hand. A set of 128 reasoning items was used as experimental materials. Nine samples (twenty participants each) of subjects participated in the experiment. The overall accuracy was about 97 percent, showing that solving these reasoning problems was well within people's cognitive capacity, which allows using introspective data. As instructed, right after solving each problem, the participant was asked to rate the perceived degree of relative difficulty of that problem on the 1–7 point scale. In the cross-validation test, over 128 experimental reasoning problems, the correlations between the perceived mean ratings, generated from one sample and that from another sample were about 0.93, accounting for 86 percent variance. This was an almost perfect result. Now, let us set up a prize of $200 to reward the best performance. The question would be how to determine the best performer in the rating game, which is completely based on self-reporting data. Accordingly, one may also ask if there is a winning strategy. The answer would be the best performer is the one whose ratings have the highest correlation with the overall means; the best strategy for each participant is nothing else but to try to do the rating most sensitively as well as consistently and assume everyone else trying the same way. We might call it "the symmetry strategy." This example might serve as a starting point to taste the invisible hand conjecture.

Once, Stiglitz (February 25, 2010) wondered, at a broadcast that given the scale of the recent financial crisis, why we have not seen this invisible hand at work. He said, "That is because it doesn't exist!" Prof. Stiglitz might be oversimplifying the issue of the invisible hand if he was serious. It should be suggestive to review what Marshall had to teach us in his classic work (1890/1938) *Principles of Economics*:

> *In economics, those results whose reasons are known or those reasons whose consequences are known, in general are not most important. Invisible thing is more valuable than "visible thing" to study* (p. 616).

Here, we assume that the terms "invisible" and "unobservable" can be used interchangeably. By T. D. Lee (1988), in physics, generally, the non-observable implies some symmetry, and the symmetry implies a special kind of conservation. By the similar principle, we may postulate that some certain degree of invisibility is needed to keep the individual market participants information symmetric, and this symmetry is necessary to achieve the conservation of the perfect competitiveness for a market. In the following, we consider different kinds of symmetries and discuss about four versions of the invisible hand implied accordingly.

The first version is to assume the individual market participants as null observers, or say, they are observers with null observations on the market. This kind of global symmetry is categorized as Symmetry 3 in Section 2.1. In this case, the conservation of the market would demand an absolute invisible hand, which can be called the Newtonian invisible hand. Here, the individual market participants are treated as the Newtonian dots, each of which only behaves based on his or her self-regard. Obviously, in this case, the individual market participants have not assumed having any market strategy so that the market is with the highest degree of information entropy, and it can yield only minimum level of wealth. This case is surely not supported by the rational expectation theory in economics as this kind of symmetry can be easily broken. Let me quote from Marshall (1890/1938) below:

Now the side of life with which economics is especially concerned is that in which man's conduct is most deliberate, and in which he most often reckons up the advantages and disadvantages of any particular action before he enters on it.

Taking Marshall's words into account, we can have the second case in which each market participant is doing non-null observations. Since the observations are non-null, it allows individual differences in viewing the market. In this case, we assume that every individual market observer observes the same market and obtains the same information from the market, although they can think of it differently. This is another kind of global symmetry. This categorized as Symmetry 1 in Section 2.1. This symmetry would require the invisible hand to treat all the individual market participants equally well or equally not well in order to maintain the conservation of the fairness of a perfectly competitive market. This is the second version of the invisible hand; it treats the invisible hand as an invariant so it can be called the special relativistic invisible hand (see Chapter 5). This version of invisible hand is surely not supported by information economics given that a great deal of robust "information asymmetric phenomenon" has been documented. To look for the next case, let me quote Marshall again:

For in the first place, they deal with facts which can be observed, and quantities which can be measured and recorded; so that when differences of opinion arise with regard to them, the differences can be brought to the test of public and well-established records; and thus science obtains a solid basis on which to work. In the second place, the problems, which are grouped as economic, because they relate specially to man's conduct under

the influence of motives that are measurable by a money
price, are found to make a fairly homogeneous group.

By taking the Marshall's words above into account, we have the third case here. In this case, on one hand, each individual market participant may have his or her different observations of the market; on the other hand, the invisible hand may treat each individual participant differently given his or her different intrinsic endowment and other conditions. Given this situation, each individual participant has to form his or her own framework on the market. In addition, each individual market participant works with the invisible hand to make the present individual connected to everyone else by establishing covariate relations. This covariate relation needs to be bidirectional such that the communication channel between the two individuals is always symmetric (this does not necessarily mean the information symmetry.) This kind of symmetry is called the local symmetry, and it is categorized as Symmetry 2 in Section 2.1. Accordingly, we may call it in this case the general relativistic version of the invisible hand (see Chapter 6).

The three cases mentioned above are not involved with the possible interferences between observations. In the next case, we want to take these possible interferences into account. Many textbooks teach us that economic analysis is more concerned with the future than the history. What one has lost is called the sunk cost. By Principle 2.1, each individual market participant is an experimenter who runs his or her own experiment. We need to postulate an additional principle before establishing the fourth case:

Principle 2.2:   Individual   market   participants   are   active
observers of the market; they have certain cognitive

endowments to observe not only the visible, but also the invisibles. Every participant is motivated to make the invisible seem visible and has certain capacity to make this possible.

Now, we are ready to build up the fourth case. When the individual market participant is making an effort to look into the future market, one is not only concerned with what happened before on the record, but also interested in observing the current observations of the other participants. Indeed, to be able to observe what others have observed would be a great advantage in the market. Let us call it the "second order observation." This is a kind of forward observation with some high degree of disturbance. Consider any two current observations, α and β. Suppose that Observation β is not observable to Observation α and *vice versa*. In other words, Observation α and Observation β are unobservable to each other. That would mean that the second order observations collectively represent a special invisibility to which Observer α and Observer β are symmetric. Nevertheless, this situation would be degenerated to the first or second cases mentioned earlier. Next, we turn to consider the case when second order observations are, in general, non-null.

Suppose Observation β is observable to the observer α and Observation α is observable to the observer β. In general, we may assume the observation of an individual market participant is observable to other participants. Let β_{α} be the observer β's observation on Observation α, and α_{β} be the observer α's observation on Observation β. It is not hard to imagine that, here, the order of observations matters. In other words, we may have

$$\alpha_{\beta}\beta_{\alpha} - \beta_{\alpha}\alpha_{\beta} \neq 0 \qquad (2.3.1)$$

It shows that the observation α_β and the observation β_α are not commutative. The mathematical framework for quantum theory is Hilbert space, in which the observables are characterized as operators. The formula (2.3.1) shows the two operators are anti-commutative because of the disturbance in observations. It can be seen as a modified version of the well-known "uncertainty principle" in quantum mechanics, first proposed by Heisenberg. Professor Samuelson, who was a great master in applying Newtonian physics in economics, wrote in his Nobel lecture (1970):

> *There is really nothing more pathetic than to have an economist or a retired engineer try to force analogies between the concepts of physics and the concepts of economics; . . . when an economist makes reference to a Heisenberg principle of indeterminacy in the social world, at best this must be regarded as a figure of speech or play on words.*

It seemed that an excellent theoretical physicist A. Zee (1986/2007) shared his idea. I admire both of them very highly. I could only blame that the present book should have been published earlier.

The uncertainty embodied in (2.3.1) implies a special kind of invisibility, which is symmetric to Observations α_β and β_α, thus symmetric to the observers α and β. This case can be named as the "quantum version of invisible hand." Different from our discussion about economic rationality in the last section, the invisible hand could not be discussed based on its internal structure as it is lacking in the literatures. Actually, to formulate the possible internal structure of the invisible hand almost signifies disclosing the internal mechanism of the market. We will face this challenge in Volume III (also see outlines in Chapter 0).

2.4 *Consumer Finiteness and Uncountably Infinite Market*

This section starts by addressing an issue concerning the mathematical foundation of the standard neoclassical microeconomic model. The issue is consumer finiteness vs. market infinity, which is sensitive to what type of experiment a market participant can run. The section will conclude by introducing a new principle that individual participants often run the Yes/No type experiment.

Standard neoclassical microeconomics is usually introduced by starting from the consumption theory, of which the central concept is *preference*. In short, we can refer to the standard neoclassical consumer model as the abbreviated "SNCM." The syntax of the SNCM starts from any given number n without telling if n is finite or infinite. Let n be the number of commodities, while X is the set of all possible combinations of n commodities; each combination within X is called a bundle. It assumes that the consumer establishes a binary preference relation denoted by "$\succ$" (strict or not strict, but always assumed as complete and transitive) on X. Then it defines symbol "$\succ$" as a continuous preference relation. Notice that the continuity in mathematical analysis is defined on the field of real numbers (i.e., the continuum), denoted by R. The semantics of the SNCM is the utility function, u: X→R. It is a proven theorem that if the preference relation is rational and continuous, then a continuous utility function exists such that $x \succ y$ if and only if $u(x) > u(y)$, where $x, y \in X$. This can be seen as the continuous version of the representational theorem in the axiomatic decision theory (Savage, 1954/1972). Thus, in SNCM the consumer is often characterized by the utility function and utility optimization.

This framework deserves some discussion. Samuelson (1938, 1948) criticized the utility explanation of preference and proposed the idea of revealed preference as the new foundation of pure theory of consumption. Arrow (1959) then provided a set theoretic proof of full preference, which had ordering based on the choice function. In the next section, we will reformulate Samuelson's revealed preference, which concerns a logical issue with the foundation of consumption theory. The issue to be addressed below is mathematical.

It is obvious that n is the number of countable commodities, which can be either finite or infinite. If n is countably infinite, which seems more likely given what the SNCM assumes, it is equipotent with the set of natural numbers N (with the cardinality Aleph 0). This will bring X (the set of all the possible combinations of n commodities) to be the power set of N (*i.e.*, 2^N). Thus, in this case, by the continuum hypothesis, X is equipotent with the set of real numbers R (with the cardinality Aleph 1), which is uncountably infinite. Note that this does not necessarily make X a mathematical field as R. For example, it is unclear on what it would mean by the multiplication of two commodities or of two utilities. To discuss any possible topological structures on X would go beyond the issue we are going to address here. What is sensitive at this point is that assuming a continuous preference relation on X would run the risk of over-modeling if this theory aims to model the individual consumer.

Notice that in microeconomics, the SNCM is supposed to model the individual consumer. A reasonable assumption is that individual market participants are likely to consider only a finite number of goods; in this case, number of possible bundles of goods being considered is still finite (i.e., 2^n, where n is finite). Some empirical research in cognitive science (Yang, Braine, & O'Brien, 1998) shows that people can ordinarily perceive three levels (or fewer) of difficulty. When more than three levels of difficulty were involved in the rating task, people would ordinarily cluster the levels of difficulty into three or less. This result is also consistent with mental model theory (Johnson-Laird & Byrne, 1990). In terms of economics, this result would imply that each ordinary consumer should be characterized by no more than three indifference curves of bundles (or goods).

Even if an individual consumer were able to think of a countable infinite number of bundles of goods, this does not provide a domain that defines a continuous preference relation, which would involve the notion of limits in terms of real variable analysis and topology. Furthermore, if X were only countable, then it would not be able to define a continuous utility function from X to R because if the domain is countable, so too must be the range (Edwards, 1965/1995).

Finally, when n is infinite and X is uncountable, even if we established a continuous utility function from X to R, it does not necessarily characterize an individual consumer with the capacity of countable infinity. This is because a continuous function may allow finite or infinite breaking points—which may possibly include all meaningful points representing the individual consumer. The SNCM is usually characterized by applying the real function analysis and topology in terms of Lebesgue measure and Lebesgue integral, which are both, unfortunately, exactly designed to resolve the difficulty caused by these breaking points. Note that the Lebesgue measure of a finite set or a countable infinite set is 0 (also see Edward, 1965/1995.)

The common misconception of the SNCM is that it treats the individual consumer as the shadow of the market; it is similar to the case of the economic rational man we analyzed in 2.2. As we have presented, that framework of SNCM is designed, from the certain perspective, to model the market rather than the individual consumer. Once we made this picture clear, one may have a better understanding about why economics textbooks often remind us that in economics, everything is associated with everything else: it is talking about the market but not the consumer. Interestingly, this idea shares some important insight into quantum theory. In quantum mechanics, every quantum state is associated with every other state and the transformation between states is continuous (Dirac, 1930/1981). In the SNCM introduced above, when n is ideally treated as infinite, X is the set of uncountably many possible combinations of commodities. Consequently, the preference relation on X can be required as continuous. Thus, we can establish the corresponding principle below.

Principle 2.3:   *Every economic state is associated with every other economic state; the transformation between economic states is continuous.*

In economic mechanics, to which this book is devoted, the notion of states is, and can only be, theory-based. Having separated the individual market participant from the SNCM, we are now ready to revisit the relation between the consumer and the market from a new perspective: as observers and experimenters, how do individual market participants participate in the market? Several issues are worth addressing here.

First, the market is uncountably infinite with continuous transformations, while individual market participants have limited observational capacities. Thus, the degree of disturbance in the observation is often high, and accordingly, the market that can only be observed as a small world. This is similar to the case in higher cognitive research described in Chapter 1. In studying higher cognition, cognitive scientists try to observe and measure the invisible mind. Here, the individual market participants are trying to observe and measure the invisible hand. Thus, naturally, we have:

Principle 2.4:   *If the degree of disturbance is high when individual market participants are trying to observe and measure the market, they often run into Yes/No type experiments* (as introduced in Chapter 1).

Second, there are all kinds of individual differences among market participants, such as the difference in capital, training (including cognitive endorsements), or position. However, the more capacities you have, it may well be the case that you have to face a higher invisibility, and probably, you would have to make more efforts. For example, just imagine the degree of invisibility of the situations that world leaders or Wall Street professionals must face. With this in mind, it is reasonable to theoretically assume as a working hypothesis that there is a proportionality constant of invisibility for individual market participants. The exact level of this theoretical constant in economics is an empirical issue. Here, I try not to make an analogy to the case of Planck's constant in quantum physics.

Third, cognitive science has provided a great deal of empirical evidence showing that there is a certain level of cognitive capacity that is shared by individuals such as world leaders, bankers, and ordinary investors. At this point, they share the same motivation to observe the invisibles, even if these seem to be non-observables, given certain constrains and criterion. In this sense, it should not be blamed on how greedy Wall Street professionals are. Ordinary individual investors share the same mentality of trying to break invisibles and to take advantages of possible information asymmetry; that is perhaps one of the reasons why people invest. The difference is that individual market participants are in different conditions and different positions; consequently, they naturally run different experiments based on different experimental settings. This situation is analogous to quantum physics, which investigates different particles with specifically designed experimental setups and carefully selected particular materials. In addition, the equipment matters; different particles can only be accelerated by certain accelerators with different levels of high energy. In Chapters 3–5, we will argue that in economic world, money represents financial energy and moves with the highest (optimal) speed.

Fourth, modern economics is a well-established scientific domain, of which the theories and mathematical models are based on facts or observable phenomenon. Here, by the facts or observable phenomenon, we used to mean they can be measured given the current empirical methods. Beyond this, all other things, even those that are economically meaningful, are classified as non-observables and are currently excluded from economic modeling. From a quantum theoretic viewpoint, many of those non-observables can also be tested and measured. Here is an interesting methodological as well as statistical issue from modeling perspectives: let us assume the phenomenon being observed is continuous. When the degree of disturbance is low, the observer is able to perform the discontinuous observation and obtain enough data points. This kind of observation can be called the *backward observation*. These data points can be connected to draw a curve, and then it can be characterized by a continuous function such as the empirical approximation function. Because such continuous functions are differentiable, we are able to characterize the margins by their corresponding derivatives. This is the technology behind margin analysis in economics. No secret, this is exactly the modeling method used in Newtonian classical mechanics, and it was successfully borrowed by classical psychophysics and neoclassical economics.

When the degree of disturbance is high and when it reaches certain criterion, the observer can no longer perform discontinuous observation. Briefly, the theory about how a system works becomes purely hypothetical. In quantum theory, this is called the "U-process," and the states are not directly observable. We can only make virtual observations and predict the results of virtual experiments about virtual eigenstates. This kind of observation in economics can be called the "forward observation." The real measurable quantities in a factual experiment are called eigenvalues; this is where the so-called "R-process" in quantum theory starts. When the number of eigenvalues is normalized to two, it becomes the Yes/No type experiment. As mentioned in chapter 1, different from applying continuous function in real mathematical analysis in Newtonian modeling, another set of mathematical tools (e.g., δ-function, general functional analysis, and complex analysis; see Chapter 11, Volume II) should be applied in quantum theoretic modeling (Penrose, 2004). The arguments given above can be summarized in Table 3. This volume is devoted to exploring the right column.

Table 3

Economics / Market	Continuous phenomenon	Continuous phenomenon
Direction of observation	Backward	Forward
Degree of disturbance	Low	High
Discontinuous observation	Possible	Impossible
Enough observable data	Enough to curve	Eigenvalue
Experiment type	Smooth	Yes/No
Empirical proximity	Continuous function	Dirac δ-function
Cost analysis	Margin cost	Opportunity cost

Table 3 can be read in three levels. The first level is the phenomenon, which in this case is continuous. The second level is observation and measurement, and the third level is mathematical characteristics. For continuous phenomenon, only when efficient discontinuous observations can be made to break into continuous phenomenon, can it be characterized by some continuous function as its empirical proximity. When there is no efficient discontinuous experimental method available, we can only perform the Yes/No type measurements, which can only be characterized by the distribution theory, probability wave function, general functional analysis, etc. (Penrose, 2004). This argument seems counterintuitive. The following speculation would be helpful to understand the reason behind it. On one hand, we have limited observational power. On the other hand, not only do we observe through our eyes, but also through our minds. The virtual observation can also see many possibilities and may discern a great deal of future potentials.

The Yes/No type experimentations are also important in macroeconomics from the policy perspective. In many situations, specifically during the financial crisis and economic downturn, the invisibility of the future economy and potential market is extremely high, with a respectively high degree of disturbance in observation for policy makers. Thus, certain monetary policies, financial policies, or economic policies can only be treated as stimuli for the Yes/No type experiment. We have learned from the global financial crisis and economic downturn since 2008 that neglecting the experimental nature of the human economy can be extremely costly. It is urgent to call for the awareness of the experimental nature of human economy. We will address this issue in Volume III (Chapters 16 and 17) as an application of economic mechanics.

2.5 *Modal Revealed Preference and Potential Market Participants*

In this section, we will first introduce the model of revealed preference. Then we will apply the possible world semantics of modal predicate logic (see Chapter 7, Volume II) to formulate what can be called modal revealed preference, which will be used to model modal states such as *must buy* or *should buy* and to characterize the potential consumer. Accordingly, two more quantum theoretic principles shall be given. The applications of modal revealed preference are also discussed as remarks.

Professor Paul Samuelson proposed the model of revealed preference in 1938, the same year that B. F. Skinner published his classic work *The Behavior of Organisms*. Here, one may taste the same scientific paradigm that is shared by economics and psychology simultaneously at that time. When a cognitive revolution of the 1950s took place in psychology, economics took another path in favor of advancing mathematical modeling methods. Classical utility theory (e.g., Marshall, 1926) was criticized because it only served as a psychology (semantic) explanation and not an observable explanation. Samuelson suggested *dropping off the last vestiges of the utility analysis* (1938); instead, he proposed the *revealed preference* framework (1938, 1947, 1948), which is introduced below.

Assume n is the number of goods being considered. Let X be the set of all the possible consumption combinations (*bundles*) of the n goods; call X the *consumption set* (think of the prices of goods). A *choice structure*, written as (β, C(-)), can then be defined on the power set of X: assume β is a nonempty family of the so-called budget sets, $\{B_i\}$, each budget set B consists of a number of bundles affordable (i.e., B is a subset of X, but here think of the prices in terms of affordability and budgeting); C(-) is a rule of choosing that maps B to a subset of B, written as C(B), which can be read as "C(B) is the set of bundles bought given the budget set B." Samuelson postulated the so-called Weak Axiom of Revealed Preference: for a given B ϵ β, If x, y ϵ B and x ϵ C(B), then for any B' ϵ β, it must hold that x ϵ B' whenever x, y ϵ B' and y ϵ C(B').

Arrow (1959) further developed Samuelson's intuitive idea of revealed preference and established the complete equivalence of the Weak Axiom of Revealed Preference with the existence of an ordering derived through a cleverly designed finite (pair of) choice function. Richter (1966) made the definition of revealed preference in terms of a consumer function. Let <X, β> be a budget space, of which X and β are defined above. A consumer on a budget space is then defined as a function h, by which each budget set B is mapped to a nonempty subset h(B), called the choice set for B. Richter went on to defining three kinds of consumers, which is beyond the point we are going to make next.

In quantum mechanics, the vectors of quantum states only have directions but are without any lengths being attached. Here, based on the notion of revealed preference, without utility being attached and without taking price or income into account, we shall have the following:

Principle 2.5:   *In the budget space, the bundle vectors are characterized by their directions without lengths being attached.*

We will argue later that from the consumer's observation, bundle vectors no longer obey the addition rule, but instead follow the law of superposition.

Let us now consider a consumer with more deliberation powers. The case can be made in five steps. First, we assume as our working hypothesis that it may well be the case that the consumer establishes some relations between budget sets and treats the budget sets as not equally related to each other. For instance, the budgets for retirement plans and for children's education as well as personal saving accounts can be seen as more closely related, while the budgets for vacation and for food as well as the personal checking accounts can be seen as more accessible from each other. Similarly, one can imagine the case in terms of the way the president of an institution considers the relations among different portfolios. This description to extend the revealed preference can be formulated within the framework of *modal predicate logic* and its *possible world semantics* (Hughes & Cresswell, 1984; Cresswell & Hughes, 1996), which will be introduced formally in Chapter 7 (Volume II.)

Briefly, the possible world semantics for modal predicate logic consists of four components: a set of possible worlds W; a binary relation R (called accessibility relation) on W; an individual domain D_i on each possible world w_i; and a value-assignment function V. To convert the language of revealed preference into possible world semantics, let the power set of X be the set of possible worlds, W, in which each budget set B_i can be treated as a possible world w_i. Then the consumer function h can be used to serve as the value-assignment function V to assign an individual domain D_i to each w_i, corresponding to the choice set. For example, $V(w_i) = D_i$ for $h(B_i)$, where D_i is a subset of w_i. Note that there is a well documented issue called the cross-world domain problem in modal predicate logic; here, we allow each possible world to have a different individual domain. The only additional thing needed here is to have a binary relation R on the power set of X (i.e., among the budget sets.) The accessible relation R can be formulated by strictly modifying (as the reflection of) the weak axiom of revealed preference: for any possible world

w_i and w_j, assume x, y ϵ w_i and xϵD_j, we have $w_i R w_j$ if, and only if, xϵD_j, whenever x, y ϵ w_j and yϵD_j. Notice that, here, R does not have to be universal on the power set of X.

Second, syntactically, we denote the revealed preference by the conditional statement, x→y, read as that x is revealed preferred to y. Symbols □ and ◊ are commonly used in modal logic to denote necessity and possibility; thus, □(x→y) can be read as, *it is necessary that x is revealed preferred to y*, and ◊(x→y) as, *it is possible that x is revealed preferred to y*. Semantically, □(x→y) is true at a possible world w_i if and only if (x→y) is true at every w_j, provided $w_i R w_j$. By the common definition, a formula is valid if and only if it is true at every possible world. It is not hard to check out that given the model we summarized in the last paragraph, when a modal revealed preference statement is valid, the corresponding indicative revealed preference statement might be invalid. Notice that the value-assignment can also be used to modify classical framework of rational preference that involves utility function.

Third, one way to understand modal revealed preference is to think of the competition of different families of budget sets. Consider the case that there are two competing families of budget sets, β_1 and β_2, which can be assumed as mutually exclusive. In this case, the accessibility relation R consisting of β_1 and β_2 so it can be seen as a partition of the power set of X. As an everyday example, consider an institution that has two departments. In this case, a seemingly revealed preference for one department may become an institution wide modal revealed preference.

Fourth, the modal preference statements, □(x→y) and ◊(x→y), and their possible world semantic models are constructed by strictly following the structure of revealed preference and its weak axiom. It is easy to check out that they are logically equivalent. However, some advantages and disadvantages can be observed. The revealed preference and its weak axiom are claimed as a behavioral model, and thus are observable. Modal preference and its possible world model disclose the relationship explicitly between budget sets, which is indeed the advantage of the so-called Kripki semantics (Hughes & Cresswell, 1984). This new description may well reflect the cognitive nature and the consumer's mental representations of revealed preference behaviors. Thus, if revealed preference can be claimed to be observable, then theoretically the modal preference state should be testable.

Fifth, by moving from revealed preference to modal preference representation, it is a turning point to move from a set theoretic model of consumer behavior to a formal model of consumer's cognition. The modal preference can be described in different modal terms to reflect the consumer's mental states. In philosophical logic of language, modal operators can be used to characterize the modal terms in natural language such as *must, ought to, obligation, have to, believe, knowing,* and even *tense.* These modal terms obviously occur often in economic consideration, and a significant amount of economic mental states (which I will refer to sub-economic level; see Chapter 12, Volume III) should be represented as modal statements. People often say, *"I must buy a new computer"*; *"you should take a vacation"*; *"I believe I ought to take a loan"*; *"I know I am obligated to pay the bill"*; or *"if I have the chance, I must prefer to take the offer from a top university over taking an offer from industry."* These modal statements all contain some indicative content such as *"buy a new computer"* or *"take a vacation."* Jeffrey (1965) characterized the second order preference by using the example, *"Prefer preferring nonsmoking to smoking."*

The crucial point is that as stated in Principles 2.1 and 2.2, as an active observer and experimenter, the consumer may hold the modal mental state (sub-economic), or turn it into action at any time. In other words, the consumer *spins* between economic modal states and economic indicative states in a sense. In quantum theory, an electron state needs to be tested at least twice, as it may spin up or down. It must be mathematically characterized by a complex number, a+ib (called the amplitude), where real part **a** stands for one test, and imaginative part ib stands for another test, and i alone may read as subjective testing or as "I" to denote the observer (Ni, 2004). Analogically, we have the following:

Principle 2.6:   *The consumer state spins so that it needs to be tested at least twice and must be characterized by a complex number in modeling.*

This principle is especially important in modeling the modern economy; modern markets provide significantly more open opportunities and individual market participants become significantly better informed with higher degree of market awareness. Developing potential markets has become a very sensitive issue in modern economics. The potential of a market partially depends on the potential participants. As an extreme case, let us consider the modern stock market. The stock market might never achieve the market clearing point in the Pareto sense. There are many potential participants, either individual or institutional, either small or large, who hold accounts with a certain amount of capital. There is also the so-called international hot money flowing around the world markets. These accounts may be inactive for any period of time but can suddenly be reactivated at the drop of a hat. These account holders are probably the most active observers of the market at all times and test the market by taking some positions as their experimental stimulus. Richter (1966) defined three types of consumers in terms of revealed preference theory: representable consumer, rational consumer, and revelation and congruous consumer. Here, we are trying to identify a new type, which can be categorized as the *potential consumer*, or *the standing-by individual market participant*. Indeed, how we define that part of the market, formerly called the potential market, is still an open problem in microeconomics.

Characterizing the potential market and the standing-by market participants is even more urgent from macroeconomic perspectives. Consider the global economic downturn and the financial crisis since 2008. The so-called confidence issue has become extremely sensitive and essential. Without mentioning the world wide efforts, the United States passed a $700 billion bailout bill aiming at increasing the liquidity of the financial system. China issued 4 trillion RMB to extend internal demands. The purpose of all of these huge efforts is to deal with the economic potentiality. Economic professionals know that predictions are made about all possibilities and consumer modal preferences, and we know that there is high degree of disturbance in this economic experiment of global scale. There are general concerns about how it would work and how to estimate the chance of success. The following is called the first principle in quantum mechanics by Hilbert (Dirac, 1930/1958):

Principle 2.7:   The real potentiality is the squared possibility.

An alternative version of this principle is given as bellow (Ni, 2004),

Principle 2.7': The real probability is the squared potential possibility.

As Feynman once stated, this principle works very accurately in quantum mechanics, though we do not know exactly why. To illustrate here briefly, consider an experimental situation **A** and some state **β** being tested; the observation shows a result with 70 percent accuracy. This can be interpreted as a probability of 0.70 by measuring. Now, consider a new more complex experimental situation, **A′**, including **A**, and the same state **β** being tested again. In this case, getting the previous result of 70 percent becomes only a possibility, the original 0.7 probability is no longer a probability, but is called the amplitude. Consequently, the predicted result by performing a new measurement should be about 49 percent. To put it in terms of correlations in statistics, which is familiar by economists and psychologists, we used to report that the result shows the correlation $r = 0.7$, accounting for about 49 percent of the variance. As an everyday example, imagine that the president asks his economic adviser about the chance of gaining success by signing a new financial policy. Assume that the economic adviser replies, saying that the chance is 70 percent, given our previous experience and the theory. If the president considers that the degree of disturbance in observing the future situation is high, he should realize that, at most, the chance of success is 50 percent.

Chapter 3

A Threefold "Isospin" of Money, Consciousness, and Light

A brief description of the term "isospin" was provided in Chapter 0, where the present chapter was outlined. This chapter provides preliminary discussions about some similarities between money, consciousness, and light. In physics, light is characterized by a set of properties or theoretical characteristics such as travels with the highest and constant speed, massless, possess energy, electromagnetic wave, and photons or gauge bosons responsible for particle interactions. I refer to these properties collectively by the term "light-like-ness." When the analogies of these properties are associated with consciousness and money, they are referred to the term "quasi-light-ness."

There are two dictionary meanings of the word "lightness" (Merriam-Webster's Collegiate Dictionary): (1) the quality of being illuminated: illumination; the attribute of object colors by which the object appears to reflect or transmit more or less incident light and (2) the quality or state of being light, especially in weight. In this volume, we will often mention about Wilczek's book *The Lightness of Being* (2008); thus, we will not note the year of his book in the rest of this book. In this volume, the term *lightness* will be used in an extended sense from the usage in Wilczek's book and meanings given in dictionaries.

In the present chapter, we mostly deal with mass and speed in the light-like-ness and in the quasi-light-ness. Section 3.1 will briefly introduce the speed of light in physics. We will analyze the conceptual difficulty of establishing the quasi-light-ness for money and consciousness, and then propose a strategic solution. The arguments to be made in this chapter will be analytical arguments. The strategy is to make consciousness and money with less and less "mass" until each becomes "massless" in its domain, such that they are able to achieve the logical possibility of possessing the quasi-light-ness in terms of their traveling speed.

Section 3.2   is about the quasi-light-ness of consciousness in terms of its traveling speed. In Chapters 12 and 14, other properties of the quasi-light-ness of consciousness will be discussed, where consciousness is characterized as mental "gluons" responsible for interactions at the sub-economic level. Section 3.3 is about the quasi-light-ness of money in terms of its traveling speed. This idea will be further discussed in Chapter 4 and modeled in Chapter 5. In Chapter 13, the monetary price is characterized by "economic photons," which is another property of the quasi-light-ness of money.

Many remarks and discussions can be made along this line of theorizing and modeling, but we will keep it rather straightforward at the present stage.

3.1 *The Light and Light-like-ness*

Einstein originally referred to the special theory of relativity as the theory of invariance. As we learned from T. D. Lee's insight (1988), any invariance implies some symmetry in physics. One of the core postulates of special relativity can be stated as: *The speed of light is invariant.* This postulate implies the symmetry that all observers in inertial frames will measure the same speed of light, regardless of their state of motion (McMahon, 2006).

As Wilczek puts it, *"Light is a most important element of 'all things.'"* It is so fortunate for a scientific field, namely, physics, to observe the speed of light:

$$c = 3 \ x \ 10^8 \ m/s$$

This equation indicates three properties: first, it is the highest speed of traveling that can occur in a vacuum; second, it is constant; and thus, third, it is limited. This third property was particularly noticed by Wilczek when relating this limitedness to the necessity of field theory of the grid. It is well known that light can be characterized as a wave (the electromagnetic wave, by Maxwell) or a particle (photon). Either way, it makes sense to talk about its velocity, namely, the distance over a time unit, which is measurable and can be determined by physical experimentation. Because the speed of light is constant and the highest, it is sometimes convenient to normalize it as $c = 1$. Thus, time and distance can be used interchangeably as:

$$1s = 3 \times 10^8 \ m, \text{ and } 1m = 1/3 \times 10^{-8}s.$$

Utilization of the normalization of c is to treat c as an identity element of mathematics. The notion of velocity is basic to physics; it can be seen as a great advantage (or say, a privilege) to physicists. The velocity $v=d/t$ is based on the measurable variables in physics: time and distance. In cognitive science and economics, there may be ways to deal with the notion of time; however, it would be a great challenge to speculate and to play with the notion of distance.

In this chapter, theoretically, we aim to analogically identify (1) consciousness as the "mental light" traveling with the constant and highest speed in the mental world and (2) money as the "economic light" traveling with the constant and highest speed in the economic world. It seems natural to do so for (1) we have a commonly made metaphor: "His thought is as fast as light," and for (2) the concept of money was described as the "Great wheels of circulation" by Adam Smith (Menard, 1978). In a sense, one might even say that consciousness is the money of thinking or that money is the consciousness of economy. But to go beyond these metaphorical sayings is hard to avoid meeting the following two difficulties.

The first difficulty is quantitative and simple: we do not even know how to measure the velocity of either consciousness or money because neither is a well-defined notion, though we may speculate on both conceptually. Strictly speaking, to have a mathematically well-defined notion of velocity is one thing; to have a well-thought-out concept of speed is another thing. The two are closely related but different. Despite the differences, they are still meaningfully related. The point is that by keeping the notion of physical velocity in mind, we can be guided to consider the features of speed in order to make sense for applying ideas of the special relativity. In addition, for the speed of consciousness, physiologists and neurologists (e.g., Damasio, 1999; Churchland,

1984/1988; Blackmore, 2003) might be able to provide some meaningful insights, if there is any. For the speed of money, there needs to be a carefully detailed conceptual analysis (e.g., Simmel, 1900/1977; von Hayek, 1976/1990; Cencini, 1988). Strategically, we will not deal with the difficulty of this quantitative kind here.

While the second difficulty seems more complex, it is qualitative so that we can find a way to proceed. This second difficulty can be stated as a question: In which sense can one say that consciousness travels with the highest (constant) speed in the mental world and that money travels with the highest (constant) speed in the economic world?

We intend to characterize consciousness and money as (i) they are always in motion; (ii) they are moving with a certain speed; (iii) they are traveling with the highest speed (i.e., faster than other mental or economic entities); and (iv) they are traveling with a constant speed. Given the obvious disadvantage in comparison to physics, we lack certain definite notions such as time and distance. This allows only qualitative arguments to be made here. The structure of the argument has to follow the schema of conditional introduction in logic: Given a set of premises $\square$, under assumption A, if B can be inferred, then from $\square$ we may infer that if A then B. In other words, what we are able to argue for are conditional statements. In the following, we will take (i) as given, argue for (iii) under the assumption of (ii). In other words, we aim to establish that given (i), it implies that if (ii), then (iii). Then, it should become more natural to make the further assumption of (iv). We will follow this strategy to solve the difficulty of the second kind, which is a qualitative issue. We will deal with consciousness in the next section, and then money in the following section.

3.2 *Consciousness and the Quasi-light-ness*

We first want to establish (i) as an axiom: *Consciousness is always in motion.* Consciousness can be created and annihilated. Nevertheless, during the lifespan of a conscious emission, consciousness is always in motion. There are countless definitions and descriptions about consciousness in literature. The one chosen below, which is well known in philosophy of mind and serves our purpose the best, is from Meinon (Aquila, 1977.) It states:

> *Consciousness is a kind of irreducible directedness being through some intentional contents toward a possible object without requiring the existence of that object.*

Here, the consciousness is characterized by three properties: directedness, throughness, and towardness. Together, they indicate that the consciousness is in motion.

Next, we need to assume (ii) as our working hypothesis that *consciousness is moving with some (certain) speed.* By (i), consciousness is in motion, meaning it is moving; we cannot speak of the velocity of its motion, but conceptually, this does not prohibit us from taking its speed into account. At this point, it would be a bit tricky to say it is moving at some measure of speed, but it seems safe to say that it must be moving with a *certain* speed.

We now want to argue for (iii) that *consciousness travels in the mental world with the highest speed.* It should be a common mental experience to all that our thinking is sometimes faster and sometimes slower (depending on the task, mode, training, and other factors). For example, if time restriction is removed from a standard educational test such as the SAT or GRE, there would be a lot of individual differences in time needed for completion. However, the speed of thinking is not the same thing as the speed of consciousness. People are able to consistently and systematically perceive the differences in the degree of difficulty of reasoning tasks (e.g., see Yang, Braine, & O'Brein, 1998). When people perceive a higher degree of difficulty, their consciousness does not necessarily slow down. Thus, it is more reasonable to ask different kinds of questions. Here, one may ask two questions. Question 1: Are there any other "mental things" that travel faster than consciousness in the mental world? Question 2: Does the speed of consciousness change (i.e., sometimes slow down, and sometimes speed up)? Let us first try to answer Question 1.

Searle (1984) summarized four features of mind: consciousness, intentionality, subjectivity, and mental causality. He also singled out consciousness as being the *"most important one."* Searle generated these four features as major difficulties in solving the mind-body problem and *"made them seem impossible to fit into our 'scientific' conception of the world as made up of material things."* We will use the same four features to serve our twofold purpose. On one hand, the four features are all mental, which will serve well to model the mental world. On the other hand, neither do we intend to solve the mind-body problem, nor to fit any mental phenomena into a neural system or into a physical world. We will take a different path from Searle's arguments. What we are interested in is developing theoretical models of the mental world that are as isomorphic as possible with the well-developed models in physics.

Here, we propose an alternative path to model consciousness. In higher-order cognitive tasks, such as reasoning or decision-making tasks, we assume all four features are involved. The consciousness does not seem to always go that fast because it is considered to be associated with the other three features. Consider the following expression: *I am conscious of that A*, and refer *A* to any putative statements, say, *something dangerous is approaching*. Let us first remove the subjectivity "*I am.*" By doing so, we can have a revised version: *Being conscious of that something dangerous is approaching*. Here, *A* involves intentionality (aboutness) and causality; let us remove *A*. What has been isolated is the phrase "*being conscious.*" This way, by separating the other three features from consciousness, we have made consciousness conceptually simpler and simpler until it has become mentally *massless*. This treatment is worth making because it does not work for other mental states. In this sense, we say that other mental states must move slower than consciousness. In other words, consciousness becomes capable of traveling with the highest speed, which validates statement (iii).

Given (i) as an axiom, under assumption (ii), we have arrived at (iii) consciousness travels with the highest speed in the mental world. It is obviously a limited speed. Now we have to consider Question 2 asked earlier: Does consciousness change its speed? For this, I do not have an answer and do not feel it is safe to speculate. Suppose the speed of consciousness changes; since we have admitted that it travels with the highest speed in the mental world, the low end of the range of speed change should still be faster than the speed of others. Thus, unless we could make a case of changing speed for consciousness and explain why that case matters to the main point, it seems that we should not hesitate to assume statement (iv) as our working hypothesis that consciousness travels with a constant speed.

After analytically establishing the quasi-light-ness of consciousness, several remarks should follow. First, when we say that consciousness travels with the highest and constant speed in the mental world (also in the sub-economic world), it is to say that the speed of consciousness is invariant. This does not preclude us from feeling certain differences of being conscious. Sometimes, we feel it is strong, sometimes weak, sometimes clear, and sometimes implicit. We might even feel the change in frequency of our heart's impulse. These phenomena should not be confused with the speed of consciousness. We know that in physics, from the wave perspective, the light presents electromagnetic waves with certain frequencies and length; the differences in frequency and length are characterized by colors in the spectrum of light. In the present book, we leave this topic as an open question without looking into it. Nevertheless, this book does study the relation between consciousness and "color" from a very different perspective. In Chapter 12 (see also the outline provided in Chapter 0), consciousness is characterized as sub-economic gluon, which is responsible to bound different impulses. In the QCD model of the sub-economic analysis, both impulses and consciousness carry the so-called color charges.

Second, there are two senses in saying that consciousness is massless. One may mean that it is massless from the viewpoint of physics, but this is true of any mental activity or mental event. Here, we have no intention to put a model of the mental world into any physical framework (not even a neural or physiological system). This is not the sense by which we use the term "massless" here. However, it is equally true that in the mental world, consciousness is probably the only mental state with intrinsic "physical" orientation. Consider the situation after some traumatic brain injury, the first thing (can be called mental) regained in the ICU is consciousness. In the mental world, by "massless," it should mean "contentless" or "effortless." Intentionality or intentional states cannot be contentless because it is defined by "about-ness" (Aquila, 1994).

Consciousness can be contentless and effortless, and it can still travel in the mental world partially due to its intrinsic physical orientation, which is unique among other things that can be called mental.

Consciousness is contentless, but no one calls it nonmental. Light is massless, but no one calls it nonmaterial. This idea seems a bit counterintuitive; readers might appreciate it more after reading Section 5.2: Denial of Newton's Zeroth Law, which is a reflection of the work by Wilczek. He regards energy as probably more fundamental than mass as the origin of matter. Here, we would say that mental energy is probably more fundamental than contents to the mind.

In the four-dimensional Minkowski space-time, which is the mathematical framework for the special theory of relativity, time is one of the four dimensions. Because the speed of light, c, is invariant, sometimes, the multiplication of time and the speed of light, ct, is treated as the fourth dimension. Feynman regards this dimension as the dimension of energy. What logically follows is that the speed of consciousness can be characterized as the mental energy that is carried by the consciousness over a unit of time. Here, it is worth mentioning of what Wilczek calls the Wheelerism: mass without mass. In this sense, we may make up a mental version of Wheelerism: mental mass without mental mass. Recall that by the axiom (i), consciousness is always in motion. Since consciousness carries mental energy, this mental energy can be represented by the mental momentum. According to Einstein, mass and energy can be transformed by the rate of speed of light squared for a static single matter.

For the third remark below, if confused, readers can come back after reading Chapter 5. Under certain conditions and assumptions, we have established that consciousness travels with the highest mental speed, and this speed is invariant. This can be seen as a mental version of the second postulate of the special theory of relativity. Accordingly, it implies two relativistic symmetries:

Symmetry 1: Other than consciousness, mental objects move with speeds that are only relative to the speed of consciousness, meaning the minds in any mental activity should observe the same speed of consciousness.

Symmetry 2: All the mental activities move in the same speed as consciousness through the four-dimensional space-time.

Here, Symmetry 1 and Symmetry 2 would seem inconsistent. Greene (Chapter 2, 1999/2003) made the following excellent explanations about this confusion to nonexperts. In Symmetry 2, speed refers to the so-called *combined* speed through all four dimensions (i.e., three space dimensions plus the time dimension). All objects moving in the universe are always traveling through space-time at the same fixed speed as the speed of light. There is a limit for the speed of traveling through spatial dimensions, which is the speed of light. Light diverts no combined speed in the time dimension, so in this sense, it can achieve the highest speed through three space dimensions. Other objects divert certain speed to the time dimension and leave less speed through three spatial dimensions. They seem to move slower than light as if they travel in a three-dimensional space, as stated by Symmetry 1. Finally, one might wonder about what we could mean by four-dimensional space-time. Recall the four features of mind by Searle: consciousness, subjectivity, intentionality, and causality. We have separated consciousness from the other three. Now, consider the other three features as three spatial (space) dimensions and time as the fourth dimension, one might be able to speculate what a mental space-time would look like. We can skip this topic since it goes beyond the mission of this book, which aims to focus on the topics that are closely concerned with issues in economics. The similar structure regarding money will be constructed more explicitly in the next section.

3.3 *Money and the Quasi-light-ness*

In this section, we aim to establish the postulate that *money is invariant and travels with the highest, constant, and limited speed in the economic world*. In other words, money possesses the economic quasi-light-ness.

The basic idea of modeling is to use common sense to consider money with its three forms, (i.e., cash accounting for the buying power, income for saving power, and capital for investing power). Here, the modeling method is twofold and consistent with the insights given in Simmel's *Philosophy of Money* (1900). On one hand, *money is not about what and how, but how much*; *the quantity of money is its quality*. Thus, the above three powers of money can be used to determine the qualitative grip of money traveling. On the other hand, also by Simmel, *money is not functional, but it is itself a function*. In other words, money shall be characterized with independent ontological status.

We can make a cognitive argument about the conceptual development of money. When a boy asks his parents for money to buy things, he acquires the sense of the purchasing power of money. When a young man gets an account to trade stocks online, he learns the investing power of money. When the man thinks of his retirement plan, he feels the saving power of money. Someday, when the man is asked about what he wants to do most, he answers, "I just want to make more money," without even thinking of any specific functions of money. At this point, we say money has achieved its independent status in conception.

As a modeling treatment, we separate money from its three functioning powers, similar to what we did in the last section (separating consciousness from subjectivity, intentionality, and causality.) We then may perform the similar line of arguments to assign the quasi-light-ness to money and establish Symmetry 1. With respect to money, we need to make further sociological, economical (in Chapter 4), and mathematical arguments to formulate the quasi-light-ness of money according to Symmetry 2 (see Chapter 5).

Now, consider an economic space-time consisting of the time dimension (shared with physics) and three spatial dimensions (i.e., with buying power, saving power, and investing power as three alternative functional candidates), through which money travels. It automatically holds that money is always in motion, but so do all the economic objects and events such as commodities, services, or exchanges. When they are treated as traveling in the Newtonian three-dimensional space, analogically, it makes sense for an object to stay in a static state, but the time never stops "flying." Now, economic objects or events are treated as traveling in a four-dimensional economic space-time; they must always move with certain combined speed because time no longer moves.

We assume, as our working hypothesis, that there exists a limit for any economic object to travel through the economic space-time. This implies that there is the highest speed, written as c^E, given certain economic conditions (as many theories in economics often do). Then by Einstein's Symmetry 2 introduced earlier, all the economic objects and events, including money, travel through the economic space-time with the same combined speed. Hence, what we need to argue is that money does not divert any combined speed to the time dimension, but every other economic component does. By modifying the words of Greene (1999/2003), it needs to be shown that money does not waste any time, but relatively every other economic thing does. These are the contents of the next two chapters. Let me conclude this chapter with a little poem entitled "Isospin":

> *The light is money and consciousness of matter;*
> *The consciousness is light and money of mind; and*
> *The money is light and consciousness of economy.*

Chapter 4

The Qausi-light-ness (Energy and Speed) of Money

This chapter aims to theoretically establish the lightness of money in terms of the properties of traveling speed. Along this line, I will deal with a number of controversies in the history of monetary analysis. I will make sociological remarks in the first section, and then economic remarks in the second section.

4.1 *Sociological Remarks*

Remark 1: Money is always in motion. As Simmel states (p. 511, 1900), *"Money is nothing but the vehicle for a movement in which everything else that is not in motion is completely extinguished. It is, as it were, an actus purus."* At this point, one may recall the famous sentence by Smith: *Money is the great wheel of circulation* (of commodities); however, it seems Smith did not explicitly spell out the nonstop nature of money traveling.

Remark 2:   Money never lacks the energy needed to travel. For any economic model, money is a necessary endogenous variable (e.g., related to price). Meanwhile, money is always the strongest and richest exogenous factor to a monetary economy. By Simmel, not only does money represent the relation of commodities, but it also largely represents the relation of persons. In turn, social relations affect economic relations through money.

Before moving on to the next remark, it would be helpful to quote from an excellent book by Poggi *Money and the Modern Mind: Georg Simmel's Philosophy of Money* (1993). In his Chapter 5, Poggi summarizes Simmel's ideas about the properties and effects of money by breaking them into four clusters of twelve properties. The summary may be lengthy here, but consider the length of Simmel's original work; it should be worth its weight in gold to many readers. The present author could not do any better than just to resummarize them below.

The first cluster is about instrumentality: "Money is the pure form of the tool" (Simmel, 263; 210), which includes:

1. Transportability (easy to transfer)

2. Concealabilty (silent and relatively invisible as the best embodiment of the notions of moveable, private, and personal property)

3. Generality (Simmel quotes Spinoza's characterization of money as "the compendium of all things" [410; 307] and

he conceptualizes it as "the unconditional terminus *a quo* to everything, as well as the unconditional terminus *ad quem* from everything" [283; 223].)

The second cluster is about impersonality, which includes:

4. Money is interpersonal. The whole collectivity is broadly defined until "it is accepted by everyone from everyone. Money is a transfer to the performance of others" (Simmel 463; 342).

5. A specific mentality (detached, cool, or neutral) is necessary to use money as an instrumental facility; a means, rather than to the commitment of an end. "Never undertake money transactions either with friends or with enemies" (Simmel, overheard).

6. Money affects, shapes, and limits a whole person to a much lesser extent than does the possession of other goods. "A money transaction implies no commitment."

The third cluster is about abstractness, which includes:

7. Money is indifferent: "It embodies that aspect or function, which makes things economic, and which is not all there is to things, but is all there is to money itself." Money makes itself indifferent to many aspects of "things economic" and concentrates its attention on their "economicity," meaning exchangeability.

8. Money is quantitative in its very essence, for it expresses numerically the interchangeability of things—it attaches itself to individual things as their price; thus it only exists in specific amounts. "In the realm of phenomena, only money loosens itself from any how to become wholly determined by its how much" (370; 279). Thus, it involves mental processes for calculation and its distinct "divisibility," which implies "exactness, precision, and rigor."

9. Money has "characterlessness" and has "knowability." We know money better than any other things without much prerequired knowledge. In modern society, as a social expression, a growing intellectualization is construed into money.

The fourth cluster is about potentiality (he "can" do something—this designates not only a future event which is being anticipated, but also an already existing state of energy, a set of psychical and physical aptitudes.)

10. Money has possibility. It realizes the possibility of all values and is the value of all possibilities.

11. Money has dynamic character. By Simmel's own words, "There is no clearer symbol than money of the absolutely dynamic character of the world" (714, 510).

12. Finally, by Simmel, money is not functional, but is itself a function. This idea is applied in Chapter 3 and will be modeled in Chapter 5.

Together, the above properties of money seem to indicate that money has all the conditions needed to travel with the highest speed in comparison to other economic things. But that would lead to only sociological arguments. Some remarks from economics perspectives must be built here as well. Simmel explained that money has largely increased the tempo of social life, but did not directly mention anything about the pace of money itself. What Simmel did postulate is that money represents the universal relations of goods and economic events at all levels. This postulate implies that any changes in the relation of economic matters at any level will make money move. Thus, money should travel faster than any other economic things or events. Nevertheless, we need to develop these ideas by transferring them into the language of economics. The remarks to be made in the next section will assign three more properties of lightness to money by briefly reviewing three controversies in the domain of monetary analysis, respectively.

4.2 *Economic Remarks*

Remark 3:   Money diverts the least of its combined speed in time dimension. Let us first briefly review the debate about whether money is neutral. This is actually a controversy between the so-called Chicago School and the Austrian School of Economic Thoughts. Both schools believe in free-market capitalism; they stand firmly against high governmental involvement of money from the perspective of policy making. Now, assume that a significant quantity of money has been newly issued in order to stimulate the economy. Friedman shows that the market will automatically adjust the overall price level proportionally in the long run (note that he did point out this kind of inflation would encourage opportunist investments, which would in turn hurt the health of economy). Lucas's research supports these findings and that this is still the case even for a shorter period. In this sense, they collectively claim that money is neutral.

In his selected work *Money, Method, and Market Process* (1990), von Mises claims that money is never neutral and that anything neutral is not money. He pictures the price adjustment as a step-by-step market process, which is dynamic. Let me try to characterize his approach by formulating an extreme case. Consider a market consisting of a set of sectors, M. Now make a partition of M, which consists of two subsets of M that are mutually exclusive, collectively exhaustive, and not empty. Von Mises points out that the price levels for the two subsets are not adjusted simultaneously, but in different steps. Let the market start its price-adjustment process in two steps. In the first step, the market adjusts the prices for Subset 1 to a new level. In the best situation (meaning another family or subset has not died), in Step 2, the market then adjusts the prices for the other subset to a new level (one possible explanation would be based on the *multiplier effect*, introduced by Keynes). Assume that the overall new price level is proportional to the original price level, corresponding to the quantity of money increased. According to von Mises, this process looks peaceful on the surface, but it is actually rather dynamic. If we look into the deep structure, it is no secret that this process often involves a great deal of wealth redistributions.

To take both approaches above into account, money is neutral (on the surface) or non-neutral (in a deeper sense) inclusively, we know that money moves twice as fast as each sector family. While one family of economic sectors awaiting for the market to favor it, money is always busy and does not waste any time. In this sense, we say that money diverts the least combined speed to the time dimension in comparison to other economic entities or events.

This picture becomes even more dynamic if we extend this process to the global economy while taking each country as a family during the 2008 financial crisis and considering the financial actions taken by governments postcrisis.

Remark 4:   Money travels with a limited speed. Let us briefly review the second controversy concerning the role of government on money. This time, the Keynesian approach takes one side, and the other side is the free-market approach represented chronically by von Mises, Hayek, and Friedman (to name a few).

The financial crisis of 2008 has caused an unprecedented increase in people's awareness of economic issues. To the observations of many ordinary people who are not in the economic profession, the following is a striking phenomenon. In economically prosperous times, governments favor the free-market approach; nevertheless, during economic downturns, governments are more likely to apply the Keynesian approach in policy making. This is disturbing to economists because both approaches are principled theories in the economic profession. Notice that in the approach introduced in Chapter 2, the human economy is experimental in nature. The policies are used to serve as experimental stimuli. Backward observation can be done by studying the historical data, but the forward observation into the future economy often involves the Yes/No type experiments.

It would be useful to roughly categorize possible ways of developing economic theories and models into three classes (in a backward order). Class 3 is to treat the government sector as an internal factor of economic theorizing. This is consistent with the public choices theory by Buchanan. Class 2 is to treat governments as an external factor or leading factor in economic theorizing. Mostly, it is to advise what a government should do to lead the economy. This is consistent with the Keynesian school of thought in economics. Class 1 is to treat governments as noneconomic factors in economic theorizing. Mostly, this is in order to tell what governments should not do in the economy. This is consistent with the school of free market led by Hayek and Friedman. These classes are by no means clear cut. The purpose of above categorizing is to identify a field in order to disclose the deep relation of state and money.

Let us go back to our discussion of money theory. As Friedman (1994) points out, in 1971, the last formal connection between money and gold was disconnected. Since then, money has become purely "state money." This is a very interesting concept, which deserves reviews from different schools of thought. Keynes would treat money as a natural resource of the government. Thus, for him, money must be a good thing. While for Friedman, money is a mischief(1994). He stands strongly against any form of inflation, but he does not deny the necessary role the government and the central bank have to play over money for a certain period. The Austrian school, from Rothbard, to von Mises, to Hayek, rigidly claims the free market of money. But notice that when Hayek (1976/2007) argues for the denationalization of money, he is actually criticizing the existing phenomenon that money is nationalized; this has been true for decades, and it is very unlikely that this will change in the future. Thus, if an economic theory aims to stand for a century long or so (should be long enough to be worth doing), it would be beneficial to take this factual phenomenon into account in its theorizing and modeling.

According to Adam Smith, money is not a commodity. Despite the differences among the modern schools of monetary analysis, almost all approaches share the view that modern money is not commodity-money such as gold; hence, it has no intrinsic value (Cincini, 1988). To the present author, this is an illusion, which is misleading. I propose that *modern money does possess a special and unique intrinsic value, and that value is the state that the money is associated with.* In other words, the state is the cost of money, and this is a socially shared cost for a given nation. Money is not free; the state economy is the price we pay for money. At this point, Cincini characterizes money as "the loaded wheel of circulation." In general, the conception of modern money can be characterized globally as a vector consisting of the weighted state/national money. By the argument above, without further speculation, we will assume as our working hypothesis that money travels with limited speed.

Remark 5: | Money travels at a constant speed. Cencini (*Money, Income, and Time,* 1988) made an excellent summary about an old controversy in monetary analysis: the dimensional approach by classical writers vs. the adimensional approach by modern writers. The classical dimensional approach claims that money such as gold possesses some intrinsic value, so it is commodity-money and should hold a dimension in economics. The problem with this approach is the so-called double-accounting of the output (Smith, 1876). As Cencini (1988) described, modern money is book-entry money. Modern writers mostly claim different versions of the adimensional approach in monetary analysis. For Smith, money is the great wheel of circulation; for Walras, it is numeraire; for Marx, it is the form of value; for Keynes, it is payment of wage; for Hayek, it should be a stable accounting system; for Friedman, the best money is the zero-rate money; and this list can continue. This volume postulates the nationality as the intrinsic value of modern money. One might wonder about the possibility of changing the speed of money by any authority. This possibility is refuted by several considerations.

According to Simmel, *"Money is the logic of relations: money expresses the relation of goods. Money itself remains stable with reference to the changes in relationships, as does a numerical proportion which reflects the relationship between many and changing objects and as does the formula of law of gravity with reference to the material masses and their infinitely varying motion."* It is constant. Once money is created, *"it lives in continuous self-alienation from any given point and thus forms the counterpart and direct negation of all being itself."* (1900). In other words, once money is created, it goes beyond the control of the creator. Why?

Based on the rational expectation theory (e.g., Lucas, 1981), for any monetary or financial policies nowadays or for any intentions to change the speed of money, the individual market participants will be capable of collectively balancing them out. This individual capacity and the collective effect are promised by at least one of the twelve properties given in 4.1 (e.g., knowability). Here, it is worth mentioning that money is an arithmetic system, which is cognitively routine. Money is one of the most thoughtful productivities that mankind has ever created from evolution, which reflects perfectly with commonly shared cognition. People might not know other things very well; they might not even know themselves well; but everyone, from world leaders, to bankers, to ordinary individuals, knows about money almost equally well.

As Simmel also points out, *"The individual amount of money is, in fact, by its nature, in constant motion."* This provides insight about another basic property of the lightness of money. We have the corollary: the speed of money is independent of the degree of its emission. It is to say that money travels at a constant speed regardless of its volume. People may see different amounts of money, and people are able to observe different ways of managing money, visibly or invisibly. We refer to this as the colors of money. In other words, like light, money has its continuous spectrum, which should not be confused with the speed of money.

So far, the lightness of money has been postulated qualitatively from the traveling perspectives. At this point, the inversion of Simmel's statement should also hold: The quality of money is the quantity of money. The usefulness of and the power for establishing the lightness of money will be seen in the next chapter.

Chapter 5

Money and Special Theory of Relativity

This chapter lines up a set of ideas to apply the special theory of relativity to monetary analysis and to economics in general. These ideas are proposed mainly for communication purposes. There is quite a bit of room for these ideas to be modified, developed, and even corrected. I believe that these ideas address meaningful issues, which should be taken into account by any alternative proposals along this line.

5.1 *Money Emission and Dirac's δ-function*

Any approach in the domain of monetary analysis that aims to go beyond the Newtonian tradition in physics from a modeling perspective should mention the quantum approach initiated by Bernard Schmitt (1982) and Alvaro Cencini (1988). In the following paragraph, I briefly summarize Cencini's idea (in italics) and use Dirac's δ-function to formulate this idea.

As Cencini pointed out, *the traditional analysis of production has been construed as an analogical copy of classical mechanics. The central concept of the quantum theoretical approach is that of emission. It provides the analysis of time with the idea that time is emitted as a quantum. This emission implies the possibility of time being "traveled" at an infinite speed and of chronologically distinct instants coinciding in quantum time.* To the present author, this seems to imply that money could possibly travel at an infinite speed, given that *the wavelike property of this particular emission is (nominal) money.* Thus, it seems to imply the "infinite speed" of the "money wave" due to *the instantaneous event that money is created and destroyed almost at the same moment.*

Now, let us fix this moment as t_0 and set the particular emission of money at this moment as x_0. The above idea by Cencini can then be characterized as:

$$\delta(x) = \begin{cases} 0, & x \neq x_0 \\ \infty, & x = x_0 \end{cases} \qquad (5.1.1a)$$

$$\int_{-\infty}^{\infty} \delta(x)\,dx = 1 \qquad (5.1.1b)$$

Together, (5.1.1a–b) is called Dirac's δ-function, which is not treated as a mathematically well-defined function in the classical sense of mathematical analysis. As Dirac noticed (1930/2004), "*Its use must be confined to certain simple types of expression for which it is obvious that no inconsistency can arise.*" In general functional analysis (or in distribution theory originally developed in dealing with Dirac's δ-function), (5.1.1b) is introduced as a well-defined *distribution*, for which (5.1.1a) is defined as the *testing function* and x_0 as a *supporting point.*

Three technical points are worth making here: first, to follow the common definition of velocity, we may replace the term "$x=x_0$"

by an infinitesimally small length $(x_0-\epsilon, x_0+\epsilon)$ and write Δx ($\rightarrow 0$) containing x_0. In this way, (5.1.1b) will return a distance equivalent to 1 (or a constant length m). Notice that Dirac's δ-function is widely applied in physics and engineering; that the right-hand side of (5.1.1b) is given as 1 is not of a mathematical requirement, but only for convenience to represent the upper limit constant for a given domain. In our context, the right hand of (5.1.1b) should represent a constant distance c^E, which represents the combined speed of money in a four-dimensional space-time. It may still be rewritten as 1 after renormalization. The exact measure of money speed, c^E, is an empirical issue for further research beyond the scope of this volume. In the history of physics, the constant speed of light originated as a theoretical hypothesis and was used as a technical convention (Woodhouse, 2006). Second, we may then replace "dx" in (5.1.1b) by "dt"; this way, (5.1.1b) would yield an energy level (Dirac did the treatment of this kind and referred to it as the Hamiltonian approach). Third, we may renormalize Δt to be zero when we consider that money does not divert its combined speed to the time dimension.

To show how Dirac's δ-function fits into the context here, we offer a modified version of a rather intuitive description provided by Griffel (1985/2002) below:

> *Consider a rod of nonuniform thickness. In order to describe how its mass is distributed along its length, one introduces a "mass-density function," $\rho(x)$; this is defined physically as the mass per unit length of the rod at a point x, and defined mathematically as a function such that the total mass of the section of the rod from a to b (distance measured from the center of the rod, say) is $\int_a^b \rho(x)dx$.*

Assume we put this rod in a field where there is a certain force on it with high enough energy to push the total mass of the rod from its two end sides to a midpoint at the center of the rod. Suppose, eventually, the total mass is concentrated at the center point. We may then imagine that the rod would become "*a wire of negligible mass, with a small but heavy bead attached.*" We may refer to this as the "rod-to-necklace" process, which can help us to accept the mathematical treatment in (5.1.1b) from the inverse "necklace-to-rod" process.

Now, let us ask: What economic concept is the best analogy for this dynamic process? The answer is money. Economically, money matters. From the "rod-to-necklace" direction, on one hand, money is massless without traditional intrinsic values as other commodities are from the production perspectives, but it carries high energy from an economic viewpoint (recall the properties of money by Simmel as summarized in 4.1). On the other hand, as proposed by Cencini, money is created and destroyed at the same moment (t_0) and transferred into other forms such as income, and then capital in almost no time $(\Delta t \rightarrow 0)$ through the modern book-entry banking system. No one would deny that money has certain influence on almost all kinds of economic events. Such a δ-function-like characteristic of money traveling can only hold in a field with certain forces, as in the rod-necklace example given in the previous paragraph. Monetary systems including book-entry banking serve as an institution in the modern monetary economy. The "rod-to-necklace" process of money is based on a universally available credit system and enforced by human users as forces. This process is only made possible by the evolution of economic states, which involves a sufficiently developed market and a great deal of human cognition and intelligence. These are content topics in the following sections and will be further developed in the later chapters about the sub-economic analysis.

Inversely, the "necklace-to-rod" process represented by (5.1.1b) helps us make sense of the idea that money can travel through a constant distance, but it may divert no combined speed in time dimension. In turn, it will help us intuitively establish some concepts of relativity theory such as an invariant interval and a Minkowski metric; it may help us speculate about how money carries high economic energy without possessing commodity-like mass.

Recall that in Chapter 1, we characterized experimentations in higher-order cognition research by the Yes/No type experiments. The similar discussions above can be extended to any domain conducting empirical research of the Yes/No type; in other words, the δ-function can serve as a characteristic function for any Yes/No type observation. Cencini's description of money is based on the Yes/No type observation of money. Consider a human participant that has solved a reasoning problem or a decision-making problem correctly. We can only observe the moment when the participant is marking the right answer. Suppose that this specific moment, say t_0, indicates that it is up to a certain point, say x_0, the participant has eventually solved the problem; nonetheless, we can only observe that the participant did something at t_0 but not at any other moment t_i. In the sense of the δ-function, we still say the participant spent some certain duration of time in solving the problem. Similarly, when we observe that the participant has marked the right answer up to the point x_0, though we might not be able to observe how the participant has mentally figured out the way of solving the problem, the δ-function provides an ontological argument supporting the idea that it has cost a certain amount of mental energy, or the participant has gone through some certain mental process. We will further develop these ideas in the following sections and in later chapters.

Before we turn to the next section, let us see another possibly interesting application of the δ-function in monetary analysis. One of the motivations for Cencini in introducing the notion of the emission of quantum time is to resolve the difficulty caused by what he calls the "neoclassical dichotomy" in monetary analysis. There is a long-standing controversy between the banking school and the currency school of monetary analysis. The debate is about whether the quantity of money depends on the prices or *vice versa*. This controversy is rooted in Fisher's equation: MV=PT, where M stands for the quantity of money supply and P stands for the price level. Given the circulation V and production quantity T, as Cencini explained (1988), Fisher's equation simply shows that *the quantity of money is tautologically defined by the price level and vice versa*. Thus, it proves no causal relationship between M and P.

Notice that Dirac's δ-function has an important property which has a wide range of implications in physics and engineering. Though the δ-function itself has only discrete supporting points, for any continuous function $f(x)$, we have

$$\int_{-\infty}^{\infty} f(x)\delta(x)dx = f(x_0) \qquad (5.1.2)$$

Let $f(x)$ be a pricing function, which is commonly assumed in economics as a continuous function, and we assume given the discussions in this section that the δ-function captures the characteristics of money emission. From (5.1.2), it would predict that price tends to take place where money is concentrated. It seems that more can be said at this point, but I would like to leave it as an open question for future discussion, since further inferences or speculations cannot be made safely at this stage.

5.2 *Denial of Newton's Zeroth Law in Economics*

Underlying Newtonian mechanics, there is a presupposition that Wilczek (2008) refers to as Newton's Zeroth Law: *Mass is neither created nor destroyed*; or say, *the conservation of mass*; *mass represents the very nature of matter.* He regards it as a profound mistake. In the Newtonian world-model, mass is so central that it *defines the quantity of matter and provides the link between force and motion.* As Cencini did in monetary analysis against the neoclassical dichotomy of money and production (including service), Wilczek argued against the dichotomy of physical reality: *The division of reality into matter and light seemed self-evident. Matter has mass, light has no mass; and matter was conserved. As long as the separation between the massive and massless persisted, a unified description of the physical world would not be achieved.* Wilczek proposes and promotes a new theory, which *sees a world based on a multiplicity of space-filling ethers* (though he recognizes the term *ether has a bad reputation*) *a totality* he calls *the grid.* I salute this idea. I will start to argue in the rest of this chapter that there is a cognitive grid that holds a monetary system as well as the human economy in general.

An interesting dichotomical analogy of (i) physics, (ii) economics, and (iii) cognitive science can be made here. (i) On one hand, in physics, as Wilczek stated (2008), *light is a most important element of "all things."* (ii) In economics, money is called the "great wheel" of "all circulations." On the other hand, as Wilczek pointed out, *there is a natural instinct to regard light as something quite different from matter, as immaterial or even spiritual.* In economics, money is often associated with what is called the "virtual" economy. Even when talking about circulation, the travel of money is always associated with monetary transactions in finance. This is an illusion. One would not deny that money has a moving value. In a three-dimensional space, if money stays in a static state, time always flies, which implies that the moving value of money is being wasted. From the worldview of the special theory of relativity in the four-dimensional space-time, time does not fly. Thus, money, as the light of economics, must always be in motion.

Because the above idea is a bit counterintuitive, here, it would be helpful to spell out the logic underlying Einstein's principle of special relativity. First, it introduces the notion of the so-called *combined speed* in the four-dimensional space-time. Second, it assumes everything moves with the same combined speed in four-dimensional space-time. Third, because light travels with the highest speed in the three-dimensional space, we can infer that light diverts the least of its combined speed to the time dimension in space-time. Thus, light can still keep the highest combined speed (higher than any others) in the "three space dimensions." Fourth, when it treats ct as the fourth dimension of the space-time, light no longer diverts any combined speed to the ct dimension (which can be seen as the energy dimension by Feynman, 1997.) In other words, light has saved all the energy to travel in the three-dimensional space.

(iii) There is a third dichotomy from the perspectives of cognitive science, but here, it is wisely addressed by Wilczek as a physicist: *We* [used to] *build our world-models from strange raw materials—signal-processing tools "designed" by evolution to filter a universe swarming with information into a very few streams of incoming data. Data streams? Their more familiar names are vision, hearing, smell, and so forth.* Here, one may add a neuron system or a computer to the list, although nowadays to mention about the limitations of the current neuron science or computer science is as sensitive as tending to increase taxes in politics. However, Wilczek concludes that *the ultimate sense-enhancing device is a thinking mind. Thinking mind allows us to realize the world constrains much more and in many ways a different thing than meets the eye. Many key facts about the world do not jump to our senses.*

Conceptually, it seems easier to capture the notions of light, money, and thinking mind in energy-like terms rather than in mass-like terms. Physicists tell us that light is massless but carries energy. Economists would not deny that money carries economic energies although money should not be treated as a commodity. A typical example is to use financial policies or fiscal policies in the worldwide economic downturn in recent years. Cognitive scientists would not deny that any cognitive efforts made in various tasks in the laboratory as well as in everyday life cost mental energies. The economic energy and mental energy are of course different kinds of energies from the energy in physics. What we can expect is that Einstein's formulas for an isolated body,

$$E = mc^2 \qquad \text{or} \qquad m = E/c^2$$

may provide us insight regarding monetary velocity as it did for physics. At the moment, we are unable to provide a quantitative account about monetary speed (which goes beyond the scope of this volume). Nevertheless, we will argue for the qualitative properties of monetary speed and intend to show why it is an interesting issue to address. In other words, we would like to explain in the next section what would follow from economic modeling perspective, assuming we had better knowledge about the monetary speed.

Monetary energy and mental energy can be exchanged easily because both are individually oriented. The human mind is an individual thing. As Simmel stated (see 4.1), money is universal in the sense that every individual uses it and accepts it. Money has the highest concentration of human intelligence in comparison to any other economic things.

By Wilczek's view, energy contributes to the physical reality of matter. I would say that mental and economic energy contributes to economic reality of modern life; here, it means the economic energy carried by money. Mental energy and monetary energy are closely related in that they flow and transform back and forth. In economics, as every textbook reminds us, all the choices are for individual participants and decisions are made by individuals. It is the individuals who formulate their monetary choices and decide how much and when to spend, to invest, or to save. In turn, no matter how limited the amount and no matter how poor or rich, it is money and moneymaking that make individuals energetic to create and to keep economic dreams, to calculate preferences, to plan and to budget, or to take actions and to take risks.

In theoretical physics, theorists have to balance between matter and space from modeling perspectives: how much weight to put on each side. For Newton, mass is central to matter, so accordingly, it assumes an empty vacuum on the space side. For Einstein, mass can be represented as a function of energy and the speed of light; accordingly, for quite a long time, he needs the ethers to be distributed in space. For Wilczek, energy probably becomes more original than mass; accordingly, he needs a multiplicity of space-filling ethers, or a grid (as he acknowledged, he *is a field guy*, 2008). In our model of the economic world, since we have put more weight on the monetary component of economic reality, it is natural and necessary to assign a great deal of cognitive ethers to fill the economic space. By assuming the multiplicity of cognitive ethers, to borrow the term from Wilczek, we suppose the resulting cognitive grid is isotropic in this chapter but aeolotropic in the next chapter. Now, we are about ready to see what the model looks like.

5.3 *Monetary Space-time and Money Cone*

In this section, we start to develop a monetary framework by applying theories of relativity. It assumes as our working hypothesis that money travels, and it travels with the highest and constant speed, write c^E, in the space-time to be given. In other words, c^E is invariant. One may find that without the quantitative measure and qualitative definition, or even without a complete description for the speed of money, some resulting ideas would still be suggestive and worth discussing. We first apply the special theory of relativity to construct a flat monetary space-time; there are many excellent references introducing special theory of relativity at different levels of academic breadth and depth. Here, the particular reference we will quote (in italic) is by G. L. Naber (2006). The application of general theory of relativity to deal with the notion of economic gravitational phenomena will be the contents of the next chapter. In connection, along the line of Wilczek's thinking, a field theory would move our context from special theory to general theory of relativity more smoothly than a purely geometric approach.

Let us rephrase four-dimensional Minkowski space-time, written as M, in monetary terms. Minkowski space-time is generally regarded as the appropriate mathematical foundation of the special theory of relativity. We take three monetary powers: purchasing, saving, and investing as the three orthogonal space dimensions and denote the basis of each corresponding coordinate by e_2, e_3, and e_4, respectively. Consider time as the first dimension; because the assumed speed of money is invariant, we treat $c^E t$ as the first dimension and denote its basis by e_1. Now, we have an orthonormal basis $\{e_1, e_2, e_3, e_4\}$. A little bit of conceptual speculation would be helpful here. On one hand, in such space-time, every point (x_1, x_2, x_3, x_4) must yield a vector from the origin by the viewpoint of field theory, assuming the metric tensor that is given. This summation is called a vector field. On the other hand, as Nabber (2006) pointed out, *it will be convenient to distinguish (intuitively or terminologically, if not mathematically) between a vector in M and a point in M (the "tip" of a vector)*; here, the points are called events. In our context, by events it could mean any economic events.

Three things are needed to set up a Minkowski space-time field: (1) a bilinear symmetric form g, in order to define Lorentz inner product and metric; (2) the four-dimensional interval and money cone; and (3) a Lorentz transformation. These are to be introduced first with a number of remarks from monetary perspectives to follow.

Minkowski space-time M is a four-dimensional real vector space, in which we can define a bilinear form $g: M \times M \rightarrow R$ that is symmetric (i.e., $g(v,w) = g(w,v)$ for all $v, w \in M$) and nondegenerate ($g(v,w) = 0$ for all $w \in M$ implies $v = 0$). Further, g has index 1, that is, there exists a basis $\{e_1, e_2, e_3, e_4\}$ for M with

$$g(e_a, e_b) = \eta_{ab} = \begin{cases} 1 \text{ if } a = b = 1 \\ -1 \text{ if } a = b = 2,3,4 \\ 0 \text{ if } a \neq b \end{cases}$$

g is called a Lorentz inner product. When g is defined as a metric tensor in a flat space-time using *Cartesian* coordinates, we have

$$(g_{\mu\nu}) = (g^{\mu\nu}) = (\eta_{\mu\nu}) = \begin{pmatrix} 1 & 0 & 0 & 0 \\ 0 & -1 & 0 & 0 \\ 0 & 0 & -1 & 0 \\ 0 & 0 & 0 & -1 \end{pmatrix}$$

with the diagonal elements $(1, -1, -1, -1)$

We may introduce the notions of the space-time *interval* and the null (light or money) cone by looking at the Lorentz inner product: a vector v in *M is said to be timelike, spacelike, or null if v•v is positive, negative, or zero. The set of all null vectors is called the null cone in M.* The figure of this idea can be found in any book about the special theory of relativity (see the figure below).

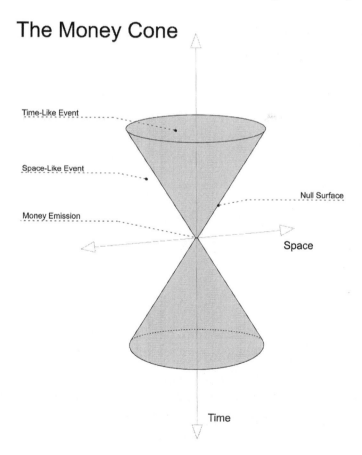

This can be referred to as the vector-description of the null cone; this is more from the viewpoint of a field. The notion of light (null) cone is more often introduced in a point-description in terms of four-dimensional *space-time interval* from the geometric space viewpoint. (Here, we adopt the wording of McMahon, 2006.) *The space-time interval gives the distance between two (point, by the author) events in space and time. The interval generalizes this notion (classical distance d) to the arena of special relativity, where we must consider distance in time together with distance in space. Consider an event that occurs at* $E_1 = (ct_1, x_1, y_1, z_1)$ *and a second event at* $E_2 = (ct_2, x_2, y_2, z_2)$. *The space-time interval, denote by* $(\Delta S)^2$, *is given below*:

$$(\Delta S)^2 = c^2(\Delta t)^2 - (\Delta x)^2 - (\Delta y)^2 - (\Delta z)^2$$

By using metric $\mathrm{diag}(\eta_{ab}) = (1, -1, -1, -1)$ and treating the term ct as the e_1 coordinate. *An interval can be designated as timelike, spacelike, or null if* $(\Delta S)^2 > 0$, $(\Delta S)^2 < 0$, *or* $(\Delta S)^2 = 0$, *respectively. Then the light (null) cone can be characterized as the lines that make 45 degree angles with* x_1-*axis, i.e., the lines that satisfy*

$$(ct)^2 = (x_1)^2.$$

The interval is important because it is an invariant quantity. The meaning of this is as follows: while observers in motion with respect to each other will assign different values to space and time differences, they all agree on the value of the interval. This is promised by the postulates of the special relativity theorem (see McMahon, 2006). This leads us to introduce the Lorentz transformation from one frame with the coordinate basis $\{e_1, e_2, e_3, e_4\}$ to another frame with basis $\{e_1^*, e_2^*, e_3^*, e_4^*\}$. This is considered as a required component of the metric tensor. The Lorentz transformation is given by four equations below:

$$x^* = (x - vt) / [1 - (v^2/c^2)]^{1/2}$$
$$y^* = y$$
$$z^* = z$$
$$t^* = (t - vx/c^2) / [(1 - (v^2/c^2))]^{1/2}$$

Given the preparations above, we are now able to analyze this from three economic perspectives.

Remark 1:   As Naber points out (2006), *In our mathematical model M of the world of events, this very subtle and complex notion of an admissible observer is fully identified with the conceptually very simple notion of an admissible basis* $\{e_1, e_2, e_3, e_4\}$, as well as the notion that *Lorentz transformations relate the space and time coordinates supplied for any given event by two admissible observers.* Consequently, all admissible observers will agree on the observations of the same emission of light as well as the constant speed. Now, let us consider the admissible observers as money users or money viewers. Analogically, they may view an emission of money from different angles and positions (i.e., different basis), that is, that they may hold different frames of combining the monetary powers (i.e., purchasing, saving, and investing) and that they view the money as it travels in the same speed. In other words, though people may well be in different positions with different budgeting strategies, they all share the same worldview about the speed of money.

Remark 2: The notion of a light cone reflects the following causal relation: only those timelike events within the "past cone" ($t < 0$) have affected the event at the origin, and only those timelike events within the "future cone" ($t > 0$) will have been affected by the event at the origin. The spacelike events outside the light (null) cone are regarded as having no causal relations with the event at the origin. To replace c by c^E, which was introduced earlier for a given emission of money as the event at the origin, we can get the idea about its money cone. Only those timelike economic events within the "past cone" have affected this specific emission of money, and only those timelike economic events within the "future cone" will have been affected by this specific emission of money. The spacelike economic events outside the money cone have no causal relations with this specific emission of money. One may find this idea provides a common sense to model the cluster's causal relations of economic events, while assuming the highest and constant speed of money traveling.

Remark 3: These equations and Lorentz transformation could only make sense when v stands for a high speed or a speed close to the speed of light. Some particles travel with a high speed or with a speed close to the speed of light. Can we accelerate a moving entity with already high speed to reach the speed of light? The answer is negative. Feynman (1997) once explained the logic for why we cannot (of course this is a trivial question to physicists). The logic is that to further accelerate an entity that is already moving with a high speed, it would demand much higher energy, which in turn will largely increase the mass; that would prevent further acceleration. In economics, there are many possible factors that affect the economy in such a way as to affect efficiency. These factors range from administrative order, regulation, legislation, policy, to war. However, these factors cannot achieve the efficiency provided by money as they can be highly costly in economic and cognitive energies, particularly for developed democratic countries.

Keep in mind that we are a very lucky generation of mankind as we have enjoyed more than six decades of world peace since World War II. This is unique in history. It should not be viewed as a coincidence that this is also a historical period that money is disassociated from gold and has more than ever played a significant role in the modern economy. Now is the time of the monetary economy. During the economic downturn today, after worldwide financial crisis, the world is facing many conflicts. The most significant one is the so-called monetary war, as nationality serves as the intrinsic value of money. If one has to choose between two kinds of war, monetary or military, which would one prefer? The wise choice is the monetary one, given that the military one is much more costly in both mental and economic energies.

Remark 4:   The previous remark actually follows the anthropic principle in physics, which states that the laws and parameters of the universe take on values that are consistent with conditions for life. This phenomenon is regarded as a necessity because living observers would not be able to exist, not to mention that they would not be able to observe the universe. This principle is still controversial in physics. However, it seems much more natural when it is applied to monetary analysis or to economics in general.

Chapter 6

Mental Ethers, Pareto Efficiency, and Economic Gravity

6.1 Curved Space-time in Economics and Why

This chapter applies insight from the general theory of relativity to economic modeling. It is appropriate to first mention, without comments, two popular books published in the last few years. One is by Thomas L. Friedman (2005/2007), *The World Is Flat: A Brief History of the Twenty-First Century*. The other is by David M. Smick (2008), *The World Is Curved: Hidden Dangers to the Global Economy*. In Chapter 5, we discussed the *flat* Minkowski space-time employed by the special theory of relativity. In this chapter, we will discuss the curved space-time that is used to characterize the general theory of relativity.

As Wilczek (2008) states, in the general theory of relativity, Einstein used the concept of curved space-time in order to construct a theory of gravity. We can describe the general theory of relativity by using two mathematically equivalent ideas: geometrically curved space-time or a metric field. On the geometric view, in curved space-time, one can imagine that the vector changes its direction and length from point to point; thus, the notion of a vector has to be extended to the idea of a tensor. For a field view, an example given by Feynman (1997) is a heated board with temperature varying at different points. Field theory is widely used in physics. There are three key concepts to the notion of a field. First, it contains something physical, economic, monetary, or mental everywhere in a continuous sense. Second, the distribution of the "thing" is in general not isotropic, but is instead aeolotropic. Wilczek argues that it also requires the aeolotropism to be spontaneous in nature (2008). Third, it has a metric because according to Einstein, space without metrics is unthinkable (1920). Based on this idea, Wilczek extends the notion of a metric field to his investigation of a metric grid (2008). The example he used to explain is a map with information of locations in terms of their aeolotropism.

So far, we have by analogy referred to the quasi-light-ness of money in terms of its masslessness (Chapter 3), energy (Chapter 4), and speed (Chapters 3–5.) By the same token, one may also imagine a field of money in terms of its luminosity, whose distribution is in general aeolotropic. By this, we mean individuals view economic events differently, or they pay different degrees of attention to economic events, from one to another and from an event to another event. In Chapter 5, we reported how commonly shared cognition makes it possible for money to travel with the highest and constant speed. The present chapter will focus more on how individual differences make the economic space-time curved. Indeed, it cannot be wrong to say that the broader the freedom to be shared, the deeper the individual differences that can be allowed, as Simmel stated (1900). This is common sense, given the notion of the free market in monetary economics.

We may now consider a general economic system, or an economic space, in which each point stands for an economic event. In the market economy, an event involves a group of individual participants. The economics textbooks always remind us that everything is related to everything else; it should be equally true to say that everyone is related to everyone else. Recall that in Chapters 1 and 2, the human economy is treated as experimental—probably the greatest experiment mankind has ever conducted. In economics, when we talk about decision making, it is always about individual decision making. This is because that decision making always involves mental activities, and the human mind is individually oriented. We propose that the economic system is always accompanied by a field of human thinking. The economic space is filled out with what we would call the "mental ethers." For a given economic event, these mental ethers involve a local neighborhood of individual economic cognitions. Let me modify Wilczek's (2008) words: the new theory sees an economic world based on a multiplicity of space-filling mental ethers. I would call this totality the cognitive grid.

In the present chapter, we will explain why tensor analysis (Section 6.3) and curvilinear coordinates (Section 6.4) are necessary from a modeling perspective when a field of mental ethers is attached to the economic system. Section 6.5 will characterize the notion of Pareto efficiency in economics by the notion of geodesics in the general theory of relativity. There, we will also enjoy an economic and everyday life version of the "happiest moment" that Einstein experienced. We will characterize what we would call the economic gravity in terms of economic curvature. Some mathematical tools are not avoidable, but we will try to make the context as descriptive as possible. Before we turn to Section 6.3, it seems necessary to insert Section 6.2 below because we have another concern with current theories in economics.

6.2 Macro-externality and Full-dimensional Individual Difference

Our concern is with the notion of externality. In economics, an externality (or transaction spillover) is a cost or benefit, not transmitted through prices, incurred by a party who did not agree to the action causing the cost or benefit. A benefit in this case is called a positive externality or external benefit, while a cost is called a negative externality or external cost. By this definition, one can see that *externality* is a notion in microeconomics; it is defined in terms of trading and pricing and in terms of the buyer and the seller. The third party is affected either monetarily or non-monetarily. We may refer to this traditional definition as micro-externality. We will argue that it is necessary to modify this traditional notion of externality to a macroeconomic version.

One externality among the most significant economic phenomena is about the fiscal policy. For example, the U.S. issued a bailout consisting of $700 billion in response to the 2008 financial crisis. It is in essence a "trade" between the U.S. government and big companies such as banks or automobile manufacturers. It is indeed a trade, though it is not treated as such, because it seems too big (say, too macro). The third party affected by this trade is every individual tax payer (collectively called the public.) The monetary costs to the third parties here are self-indexing; it is the whole price of $700 billion plus operational costs. We refer to this phenomenon as an example of *macro-externality*, which also has significant nonmonetary effects on the third party, which in this case we will call the "state of mentality," or the "collective mental economic state." The notion of the state of economic mentality is sensitive because it is directly related to what people used to call the *potential market*, which is exactly what the bailout money aims to stimulate.

It is worth noting that there have been two rounds of significant macroeconomic mentality build-ups since the 1990s. The first round happened during the "dot-com" bubble years, which is still fresh in the minds of those affected. Given the advancement of the Internet, the entry barrier to the stock market was nearly eliminated. This was unthinkable to old generations. Suddenly, almost every individual became a market participant. People began to dream of ways to quickly gain fortune. Every individual participant in the market felt like an authority and told others how to invest. This is a kind of economic mental state built up globally and universally. When the financial market crashed, this universal mentality remained.

The second round happened from the recent world financial crisis in 2008. This time, ordinary people started to feel that no one in the world, including national or world leaders, bankers, and economists knew any better than they did about the inner workings of the global economy. This has been a very embarrassing situation as the public came to believe that all the authorities in economics were suddenly lost. And while the economy has continued to slowly recover, this global economic mentality remains.

As a result, from the micro-perspective, the bailout has achieved the unprecedented individual divergence in economic thinking. People no longer ask what your country can do for you but instead ask what you can do for yourself. This is based on the personal endowment of economic resources. From a macro-perspective, each country or region has become more self-oriented and this makes the global economy a more curved place. To mathematically characterize this phenomenon, in the next two sections, we will show that tensor analysis and the local frame of curved coordinates are necessary mathematical tools to apply.

6.3 *Economic Polarizability: the Invisible Hand as a Tensor*

We assume, as our working hypothesis, that people have different views toward any given economic event, and that they pay different degrees of attention or spend different amounts of mental energy on any given economic event. We further assume that for any given individual, one may have inconsistent views toward different economic events, and one pays different degrees of attention or spends different amounts of mental energy on them. In this sense, we say that the mental ethers are the economic space-filling item (in Wilczek's terms, 2008). Mental ethers are in general not isotropic or uniformly distributed, but are aeolotropic everywhere. To analyze the aeolotropism of mental ethers, we can utilize tensor analysis. Tensor analysis is a mathematical tool which can be introduced through examples either in terms of geometry or physics.

To introduce the notion of a tensor, we may first consider electric polarizability in physics (which can be referenced from any textbook or by utilizing the internet) as an example, and then analogously introduce the notion of *economic polarizability*. Economic polarizability is a new concept being formally introduced in this volume. We need to distinguish between two cases: when the electric medium is treated as isotropic and when it is treated as aeolotropic (asinotropic). polarizability is a property of matter. Polarizability determines the dynamical response of a bound system to external fields, and provides insight into its internal structure. In case of the electric medium that is isotropic, the electric polarizability α is defined as the ratio of the induced dipole moment P of an atom to the electric field E,

$$P = \alpha E \qquad\qquad (6.3.1)$$

Two points are worth noting here. First, for any given unit area or for a point in a three-dimensional space, the electric dipole moment P and electric field intensity E are two vectors (namely, tensors of rank 1.) Second, the dielectric is isotropic, vectors P and E share the same direction and the polarizability α is defined as a scalar quantity. The fact that it is a scalar quantity does not affect the shared direction of P and E, but rather only determines the proportional relation between the corresponding components P_i and E_i ($i = 1, 2, 3$) in P and E.

Given the above insight, conceptually, we may generalize the notion of economic polarizability. The above case can be seen as corresponding to the various multiplier effects in economics including the money multiplier, fiscal multipliers, and Keynesian multiplier effects. In this case, the distribution of mental ethers, which are assumed as the economic medium, is isotropic. In monetary macroeconomics and banking, the money multiplier is used to measure how much the money supply increases in response to a change in the monetary base. The fiscal multiplier is used to analyze the effect of either fiscal policy, exogenous changes in spending, or aggregate output. Keynesian multipliers are used to measure the effect on aggregate demand in response to an exogenous change in spending. A monetary or a fiscal policy is used to simulate a particular economic state, and that will form some expected field in which at each point will be exemplified as a vector with a degree of certain intensity and with an intended direction. At this point, we suppose the response vector in the economy shares the same direction as predicted with the polarization and that this is in accord with the expected effect by the economic multiplier theories. This way, the relation between the stimuli vector (written as S) and response vector (written as R) shall be treated as a kind of economic polarizability, characterized by the corresponding multiplier α. For example, in the dynamic case,

Keynesian polarizability can be calculated by a single multiplier equation, which contains a time variable t. Notice again that the above analogy is based on the assumption that mental ethers as the economic medium in economic space are isotropic, which can be seen as a special case.

When the electric medium is isotropic, the polarizability $\boldsymbol{\alpha}$ is a scalar quantity, which implies that the applied electric field can only produce polarization components parallel to the field. However, when the electric medium is aeolotropic, an electric field in the x-direction may produce a y or z component in vector $\boldsymbol{P}$. In this case, the (linear) polarizability has to be characterized by a tensor. Let us try to introduce the notion of rank 2 tensor in the three-dimensional space as an example. Consider two vectors (rank 1 tensors) $\boldsymbol{P} = (P_x, P_y, P_z)$ and $E = (E_x, E_y, E_z)$. It is more convenient to understand the tensor relating the two vectors in terms of their components, and rewrite $\boldsymbol{P} = (P_x, P_y, P_z)$ by $\boldsymbol{P} = (P_1, P_2, P_3)$ and $E = (E_x, E_y, E_z)$ by $E = (E_1, E_2, E_3)$. When the electric medium is aeolotropic, the linear relation between $\boldsymbol{P}$ and E can be represented in terms of their components in three linear equations:

$$P_1 = \alpha_{11}E_1 + \alpha_{12}E_2 + \alpha_{13}E_3$$
$$P_2 = \alpha_{21}E_1 + \alpha_{22}E_2 + \alpha_{23}E_3$$
$$P_3 = \alpha_{31}E1 + \alpha_{32}E_2 + \alpha_{33}E_3$$

Or write as

$$P_i = \textstyle\sum_{j=1}^{3} \ \alpha_{ij}E_j \ (i = 1, 2, 3)$$

Here, α_{ij} has two subscripts, so it is of rank 2; in the case above, it is a three-by-three matrix containing nine elements (n^2).

In economics, it is not too hard to accept the concept of a stimulus vector. For any monetary or fiscal policy, say hundreds of billions of dollars in bailout money, the policy will have a predicted direction, a quantity component, and an expected time component. Usually, there are a few other components that need to be taken into account. For the time being, if one would feel more comfortable dealing with traditional multiplier effects, you may neglect other components by taking them as null components. It is now easier to accept the concept of the response vector. Given our assumption that the mental ethers as an economic medium are aeolotropic, the response vector in general is not parallel to the direction of the stimulus vector, and it may yield different component values that are not proportional to their corresponding components in the stimulus vector. This view is also consistent with the rational expectation theory and its falsifications. Thus, in case that the mental ether medium is aeolotropic, α_{ij} $(i, j = 1, \ldots,$ n) should be used to characterize the relation between the stimuli vector and its corresponding response vector for a chosen number n of dimensions.

However, α_{ij} alone does not accomplish a tensor of rank 2. Actually, a_{ij} is only one part of a tensor. By definition, a rank 2 tensor must have another part, which is the transformation rule from one coordinate basis to another. In other words, a tensor should be invariant, despite any particular coordinate basis. This is particularly important to us. As we mentioned in Chapter 5, each coordinate basis represents an admissible observer. We want to observe that all the individual market participants are symmetric to the same economic polarizability.

Consider any given economic stimuli vector $S=(S_1, S_2, S_3)$ and a corresponding response vector $R=(R_1, R_2, R_3)$. Write R_i ($i=1, 2, 3$) to denote the three numbers for the three components in the current basis $\{e_i\}$. Now, consider a new basis $\{e_{i'}\}$. We know, through the basis transformation rule, the basis component $e_{i'}$ can be represented in the current basis as:

$$e_{i'} = \sum_{i=1}^{3} A_{i'i}\, e_i$$

If it follows the same transformation, and becomes

$$R_{i'} = \sum_{i=1}^{3} A_{i'i}\, R_i,$$

we say R_i ($i=1, 2, 3$) is a tensor of rank 1. Likewise, S_i ($i=1, 2, 3$) can be treated as another rank 1 tensor, with transformation rule represented by

$$S_{j'} = \sum_{j=1}^{3} A_{j'j}\, R_j$$

Thus, the transformation rule for representing α_{ij} in a new basis $\{e_{i'}\}$ can be given as follows:

$\alpha_{i'j'} = \sum_{i=1}^{3} \sum_{j=1}^{3} A_{i'i} A_{j'j} \alpha_j$ Together with this transformation rule, *aij* becomes a tensor of rank 2 (as it has two subscripts), which is an invariant, independent of any particular frame of coordinates. This completes our introduction to the very basic idea of tensor analysis. As we introduced earlier, the economic polarizability must be characterized as a tensor but not a scalar quantity, where the mental medium is aeolotropic. In this case, the economic response vector may go in unpredicted directions and can yield unexpected components.

In this section, one can see that at the level of economic analysis we can treat the mental medium as isotropic. *Prima facie*, the multiplier effects support monetary or fiscal policies in a limited sense. At the deeper levels, taking the aeolotropism of the mental medium into account, the invisible hand works like a tensor. This invisible hand does not favor any specific individual market participant but instead makes them symmetric. The transformation rule promises that the polarization is an objective economic phenomenon, which is independent of any observers though they may view it differently. The rank of a tensor can be higher than 2, if one is interested in looking into more complex economic issues.

Another theoretical issue, which should not be taken as an accident, is worth mentioning here: tensor analysis is related to probability theory. As Lucien Hardy elegantly characterized (2004), the degree of freedom K is defined as the minimum number of measure probabilities to determine a state, and the dimension number N is defined as the number of states that can be distinguished by one measuring test. In this way, both classical mechanics and quantum mechanics can be viewed as probability theories. For classical Newtonian mechanics, $K = N$; for quantum mechanics, $K = N^2$. Hence, when the economic polarization is characterized by a tensor of rank 2, the degree of freedom may achieve a quantum theoretic level. In turn, as we explained in Chapters 1 and 2, the degree of disturbance to the permissible observers becomes higher, and accordingly, the economic world they can observe becomes smaller. In other words, many economic quantum fluctuations occur beyond the observational power of individual market participants. This reflects the experimental nature of human economy. Thus, each policy vector can be treated as a measurement vector.

When a global economic polarization results in national or regional economic polarizations, the possible transformations would make the degree of freedom increase exponentially. This can yield a new compound polarization, which may achieve the degree of freedom of K^2. If this process continues, like an economic nuclear process, it would cause the grip of the invisible hand to quiver, which in turn would cause the "monetary light" to curve, demand further administrative disturbance, and contribute more energy to political or even military events. This means the permissible observers or individual market participants change their straight way to think through or lose their straight vision to view through the economic space-time. There is probably too heavy of a fog as each nation or each individual is concerned with her own safety. Given the experimental nature of human economy, as the experimenters, the individual participants may feel overloaded by the living data. From a mathematical perspective, it implies that the observers have lost their frame of universal straight coordinates and turned to form their own local coordinates. Einstein introduced tensor analysis using examples in geometry, such as quadratic surfaces. The next section will elaborate on this concept.

6.4 *Economic Space with Local Curvilinear Coordinates*

It is not hard to imagine that huge economic events make the economic space curved. Since the global financial crisis began in 2008, each country or region has initiated all kinds of monetary or fiscal policies to protect its own economy. During the economic downturn, each individual has become more concerned about personal or family welfares instead of general social needs. Our working hypothesis is that people may have different views toward an economic event, and each individual may have different views toward different events. We want to speculate when the Cartesian frame of straight coordinates collapses, how the individual constructs a local curvilinear coordinate system.

Consider an affine space, in which each point represents an economic event. (This is different from Chapter 5, where each point in Minkowski space-time represents an admissible observer.) For a given event E, the individual needs to first determine the number of features to be taken into account. Let us say, three, for the time being, write @1, @2, @3. Now consider a small connected neighborhood of E; for any neighboring events, every individual takes the same three features into account. This way, the individuals have turned the three features into three variables, written as X_1, X_2, X_3. Now, we can connect three features by a linear function x_α. Because three variables are involved here, three such functions are needed in order to secure a solution. Write them as:

$$x_\alpha = x_\alpha (X_1, X_2, X_3) \ (\alpha = 1, 2, 3)$$

Here, x_α are continuous, differentiable, and single-value functions. If the inverse functions

$$X_i = X_i (x_1, x_2, x_3) \ (i = 1, 2, 3)$$

are also continuous, differentiable, and single-valued, we say x_α ($\alpha = 1, 2, 3$) sets up a local curvilinear coordinate system in the neighborhood of E. By the same token, X_i ($i = 1, 2, 3$) can be seen as another local curvilinear coordinate system in the neighborhood of E, and the transformation between the two is self-obtained by the definition. Likewise, because any other curvilinear coordinate systems are linearly dependent on x_α, the general transformation rules hold.

For any given point M in the connected neighborhood, it yields a tangent direction along each curved coordinate. Because the point has direction, we can calculate the corresponding partial derivative. We also have the useful property that states that:

$$\partial x_\alpha / \partial x_\beta = \Sigma^3_{i=1} (\partial x_\alpha / \partial X_i)(\partial X_i / \partial x_\beta)$$

$$= \delta_{\alpha\beta} = \{ \begin{array}{l} 1, \ \alpha = \beta \\ 0, \ \alpha \neq \beta \end{array}$$

This property enables us to construct the coordinate's basis and form the so-called local frame of curved coordinates.

Given the basic ideas briefly introduced above, we have shown the rough picture about the so-called *manifold* in differential geometry. An individual's knowledge about space structures can go deeper and deeper with each step. For any given point in a manifold, one can define a tensor. For any two given points, we may also define the *connection* between the two corresponding tensors. The connection is called affine connection space. Furthermore, if a non-degenerative metric tensor is introduced, we will obtain Riemann space, which is the space that Einstein used in his general theory of relativity.

Given the insights and tools that we may use from the general theory of relativity, we can look at economic space. With a cognitive field being attached to economic space, there are predictably going to be many interesting stories. These stories would go beyond the scope of this volume, and we leave the possibilities open here for more careful thinking in the future. Nevertheless, one story is essential, which will be described and reviewed in the next section. We will characterize the concept of Pareto efficiency in economics in terms of the notion of geodesics. From the general theory of relativity, geodesics can be used to describe economic curvature and economic gravity.

6.5 *Pareto Efficiency, Geodesics, and Economic Gravity*

Both the notions of Pareto efficiency and geodesics are extreme cases, which are essential concepts in their home disciplines. If they can be matched analogically, it will serve as a bridge between economics and the general theory of relativity. Let us first examine the concept of geodesics.

In the general theory of relativity, geodesics are defined by a second order differential equation with a connection as a coefficient, which we are not going to be getting into. Instead, the notion of geodesics can be viewed in a much more intuitive way. In a flat space, the geodesic is the straight line connecting two points with the shortest distance. In a curved space, the geodesic curve between two points can be seen as an arc. Here, the geodesic curve is not characterized best in terms of the distance, but instead, in terms of the tangent vector. Similar to the case for a straight line from another perspective, the geodesic curve is best characterized when all the tangent vectors along the curve are parallel. Between any two points, the geodesic curve is unique.

We now turn to review the notion of Pareto efficiency in economics. Its formal definitions can be found in any textbook or easily referenced online. Pareto efficiency, also known as Pareto optimality, is mathematically characterized in terms of allocations of goods or resources and individual utility. In a more behavioral manner, it is defined in terms of so-called Pareto frontiers, along which all consumers are assumed to share the same marginal rate of substitution. In a perfect competitive market, given the initial allocation of goods, a change to a different allocation that makes at least one individual better off without making any other individual worse off is called a *Pareto improvement*. A market state, namely, an allocation, is defined as Pareto-efficient when no further Pareto improvement can be made. Being in a Pareto-efficient state implies that the equilibrium condition for market clearance exists. We can characterize the notion of Pareto efficiency in terms of geodesics in two ways.

One way is to treat the Pareto-efficient state as a singularity point in the market space. Though it is not connected to any other state points, it can be seen as being connected to itself. The arc line from the Pareto-efficient point to itself has a length of zero. In tensor analysis, it is called an *isotropic geodesic*, meaning that a geodesic that has lost its direction.

Another way is to line up all the individual market participants. Since Pareto efficiency does not make any statement about equality or overall well-being of a society, given the general individual differences in personal endowments, we can assume the line of individual utilities is a curve. Let us call this curve a *Pareto path* within the Pareto-efficient state. Under this state, we can reasonably assume that individuals think in different directions in order to become better off or at least earn a fair share. This supposition allows us to yield a tangent vector at each utility point along the Pareto path. However, since no one can make a move without breaking the Pareto-efficient state, the length of each tangent vector here can only be zero. In this way, every tangent vector on the Pareto path is degenerated to an isovector (null vector); therefore, they are all parallel. In this sense, by the characterization of geodesics given earlier, we say the Pareto-efficient state can be characterized as the *economic geodesic*.

Both ways above seem counterintuitive, if not confusing. But let us think of situations in our daily life. When a friend or a colleague asks someone, "How are you doing?" you often hear the response "Same old, same old." What would that mean if one is in a three-dimensional space, where time is passing by? Every day is a new day. If one is in a four-dimensional space-time, as we mentioned in Chapter 5, because time no longer moves, everything must always be in motion. What that conversation means in terms of common sense is that the semester is moving very fast. We are too busy in our day-to-day lives, so we feel as if they are merging into one day, the same old days. In other words, our feelings do not distinguish between these days.

Consider one more example in our ordinary life. Someone used to work from nine to five every working day. It is your dream profession, and you greatly enjoy the job. If people say that you just work for money, you might reply that "This is my career." What is the difference between the call of duty and your willingness (or desire) to work? They are different matters, but often, we simply do not distinguish them.

In the history of science, there is a well-known story called the Einstein's "happiest moment." Einstein was puzzled over the

Newtonian notion of inertial frames for quite a while. In solving this puzzle, he first derived the following equation:

$$(acceleration) = \frac{(gravitational\ mass)}{(inertial\ mass)} \times (intensity\ of\ the\ gravitational\ field)$$

Einstein then made the following analysis (1916): "*If now, as we find from experience, the acceleration is to be independent of the nature and the condition of body and always the same for a given gravitational field, then the ratio of the gravitational to the inertial mass must likewise be the same for all bodies. By a suitable choice of units we can thus make this ratio equal to unity. We then have the following law: The gravitational mass of a body is equal to its inertial law.*" This is called Einstein's equivalence principle in his general theory of relativity.

I, myself, am convinced that what confused Einstein is analogically similar to what would make us feel counterintuitive in treating Pareto efficiencies as economic geodesics. We will discuss this further in a later chapter, which is about what I call ordinary rationality and Wittgenstein's idea about subjective certainty. Here, I leave readers to get a glimpse at the comparisons and analogies above. From the above formula and what Einstein concluded, we may read out in economic terms that the acceleration in our economic life is equivalent to the intensity of some "economic gravitational field." But what is an "economic gravitational field?"

In the general theory of relativity, the intensity of the gravitational field is defined in terms of the notion of curvature, which involves massive mathematics. For our purpose here, the intuitive description by Feynman (1997/2004) should be enough: *Curvature is the difference between measured results and the geodesics.* As we all know, a Pareto-efficient state is an ideal economic state. One of the reasons why it is theoretically useful is that the notion of Pareto efficiency tells us what is economically inefficient and why we need to make Pareto improvements. Allow and Debreu mathematically demonstrated that a free-market system will lead to a Pareto-efficient outcome, which is called the *first welfare theorem.* The theorem assumes a number of strong conditions, which can hardly be satisfied in any actual economy or by any real market. In this sense, we say the difference between a measurable economic or market state and the ideal Pareto-efficient state (which one may call a Pareto economic geodesic) is the curvature for that measured state. Because we assume any real, sufficiently active free market can never achieve the Pareto-efficient state, economic curvatures exist everywhere. This, in turn, forms what we shall call the economic gravitational field. This also means the economic space-time is curved everywhere.

Before ending this chapter, one may ask: what about the "same old, same old" experiences? Unfortunately, that is counted as the sunk cost in our economic life, which will be discussed in Chapter 15 (Volume II). Keep in mind that the current economics is about new opportunities or something additional, specifically additional per unit to be accelerated; that is the core idea of marginal analysis. Given what we have lectured so far, all individual market participants are non-inertial systems that should be governed by the same economic law: the intensity of economic gravity accelerates people's extra economic efforts. This, in turn, it holds what we may call the economic version of Einstein's equivalence principle: within a small economic space, the mental measurements of what one is used to doing constantly and what one is demanded to do are not distinguishable, so they can be treated as equivalent to each other from a cognitive perspective.

Bibliography

Allwein, G., Yang, Y., and Harrison, W. L. 2011. "Qualitative decision theory via channel theory." *Logic and Logical Philosophy*, Vol. 20.

Aquila, Richard E. 1977. *Intentionality: A Study of Mental Acts*, the Pennsylvania State University Press.

Barrow, John D (editor), Davies, Paul C. W. (editor), and Harper, Jr., Charles L. (editor). 2004. *Science and Ultimate Reality: Quantum Theory, Cosmology and Complexity*, Cambridge University Press.

Blackmore, Susan. 2003. *Consciousness: An Introduction,* Hodder Healine Group.

Braine, Martin D. S. 1998. Steps toward a mental-predicate logic. In Braine & O'Brien (editors), *Mental Logic*, Lawrence Erlbaum Associates.

Braine, Martin D. S. and O'Brien, David P. 1998. *Mental Logic*, Lawrence Erlbaum Associates.

Camerer, Colin F. 2003. *Behavioral Game Theory: Experiments in Strategic Interaction*, Princeton University Press.

Cencini, Alvaro. 1988. *Money, Income, and Time: A Quantum-Theoretical Approach*, Printer Publishers Limited, London.

Churchland, Paul M. 1984/1988. *Matter and Consciousness*, MIT Press.

Dirac, P. A. M. 1930/2005. *The Principles of Quantum Mechanics*, Oxford University Press.

Einstein, Albert. 1916/2010. *Relativity: The Special and General Theory*, BN Building.

Einstein, Albert. 1921/1953. *The Meaning of Relativity*, Princeton University Press.

Einstein, Albert. 2011. *Relativity, the Special and the General Theory*, Empire Books.

Feynman, Richard P. 1997. *Six Not-So-Easy Pieces: Einstein's Relativity, Symmetry and Space Time*, Perseus Publishing.

Ford, Kenneth W. 2004. *The Quantum World: Quantum Physics for Everyone*, Harvard University Press.

Frankel, Sally Herbert. 1977. *Money: Two Philosophies: The Conflict of Trust and Authority*, Basil Blackwell, Oxford.

Friedman, Milton. 1994. *Money Mischief: Episodes in Monetary History*, Harcourt Brace & Company.

Gigerenzer, Gerd and Todd, Peter M. 1999. *Simple Heuristics That Make Us Smart*, Oxford University Press.

Greene, Brian. 1999. *The Elegant Universe*, W. W. Norton & Company, Inc.

Greene, Brian. 2004. *The Fabric of the Cosmos*. Alfred A. Knopf.

Greiner, Walter. 1981/1990. *Relativistic Quantum Mechanics: Wave Equations (Third Edition)*, Springer-Verlag.

Griffel, D. H. 1981/2002. *Applied Functional Analysis*, Dover Publications, Inc.

Haken, Hermann. 1987. *Information and Self-Organization*, Springer.

Halpern, Paul. 2004. *The Great Beyond: Higher Dimensions, Parallel Universes, and the Extraordinary Search for a Theory of Everything*, John Wiley & Sons, Inc.

Hawking, S. 1988/1996. *A Brief History of Time*, Bantam Books.

Hawking, S. 2001. *The Universe in a Nutshell*, Bantam Books.

Hayek, F. A. 1976/2007. *Denationalisation of Money: The Argument Refined*, The Institute of Economic Affairs.

Hirshleifer, Jack, Glazer, Amihai, and Hirshleifer, David. 2005. *Price Theory and Applications: Decisions, Markets, and Information*. Cambridge University Press.

Hughes, G. E. and Cresswell, M.J. 1968/1982. *An Introduction to Modal Logic*, Methuen.

Hughes, G. E. and Cresswell, M. J. 1984. *A Companion to Modal Logic*, Methuen & Co. Ltd.

James, William. 1890/2007. *The Principles of Psychology*, Cosimo Classics.

Jeffrey, Richard C. 1965/1990. *The Logic of Decision*, The University of Chicago Press.

Johnson-Laird, P. N. 1983/1987. *Mental Models: Towards a Cognitive Science of Language, Inference, and Consciousness*, Cambridge University Press.

Joyce, James M. 1999. *The Foundations of Causal Decision Theory*, Cambridge University Press.

Kahneman, Daniel and Tversky, Amos. 2000. *Choices, Values, and Frames*, Cambridge University Press.

Kahneman, Daniel, Slovic, Paul, and Tversky, Amos. 1982. *Judgment under Uncertainty: Heuristics and Biases*, Cambridge University Press.

Khinchin, A. I. 1957. *Mathematical Foundations of Information Theory*, Dover Publications, Inc., New York.

Lee, T. D. 1981. *Particle Physics and Introduction to Field Theory*, Harwood Academic.

Lee, T. D. 1988. *Symmetries, Asymmetries, and the World of Particles*, University of Washington Press.

Li, M. 2005. *A History of Superstring* (Chinese edition). Peking University Press.

Liu, Lianshou and Zheng, Xiaoping. 2008. *Tensor Analysis in Physics*, China Science Press.

Maartens, R. 2006. Brane Worlds. (eds.) Francoise, Jean-Pierre, Naber, Gregory L. and Tsun, Tsou Sheung. 2007. *Encyclopedia of Mathematical Physics*, Elsevier Inc.

Manktelow, Ken. 1999. *Reasoning and Thinking*, Psychology Press.

✓
Marshall, Alfred. 1890/2010. *Principles of Economics*, Nabu Press.

McMahon, David. 2005. *Quantum Mechanics Demysified*, The McGraw-Hill Companies, Inc.

McMahon, David. 2006. *Relativity Demystified*, The McGraw-Hill Companies, Inc.

McMahon, David. 2008. *Quantum Field Theory Demystified*, The McGraw-Hill Companies, Inc.

McMahon, David. 2009. *String Theory Demystified*, The McGraw-Hill Companies, Inc.

Mirowski, Philip. 1989. *More Heat than Light: Economics as Social Physics as Nature's Economics*, Cambridge University Press.

Naber, G.L. 2006. Introductory Article: Minkowski Spacetime and Special Relativity. (eds.) Francoise, Jean-Pierre, Naber, Gregory L. and Tsun, Tsou Sheung. 2007. *Encyclopedia of Mathematical Physics*, Elsevier Inc.

√ Niehans, JÜRG. 1994. *A History of Economic Theory: Classic Contributions, 1720–1980*, The John Hopkins University Press.

Osborne, Martin J. and Rubinstein, Ariel. 1994. *A Course in Game Theory*, The MIT Press.

√ Pais, Abraham. 1986/1988. *Inward Bound: Of Matter and Forces in the Physical World*, Oxford University Press.

Penrose, Roger. 1989. *The Emperor's New Mind: Concerning Computers, Minds and the Laws of Physics*, Oxford University Press.

√ Penrose, Roger. 1997/2000. *The Large, the Small and the Human Mind*, Cambridge University Press.

Penrose, Roger. 2004. *The Road to Reality: A Complete Guide to the Laws of the Universe*, Alfred A. Knopf.

√ Poggi, Gianfranco. 1993. *Money and the Modern Mind: Georg Simmel's Philosophy of Money*, University of California Press.

Randall, Lisa. 2005/2006. *Warped Passages*, Harper Perennial.

√ Ross, Don. 2005. *Economic Theory and Cognitive Science: Microexplanation*, The MIT Press.

Rubinstein, Ariel. 1998. *Modeling Bounded Rationality*, The MIT Press.

Samuelson, Paul A. 1938. "A Note on the Pure Theory of Consumer's Behavior" *and* "An Addendum," *Economica*, February 1938 and August 1938.

Samuelson, Paul A. 1948. "Consumption Theory in Terms of Revealed Preference," *Economica*, November 1948.

Richter, Marcel K. 1966. "Revealed Preference Theory," *Econometrica*, Vol. 34 No. 3, July 1966.

Savage, Leonard J. 1954/1972. *The Foundations of Statistics*, Dover Publications, Inc.

Searle, John R. 1984. *Minds, Brains, and Science*, Harvard University Press.

Searle, John R. 2001. *Rationality in Action*, The MIT Press.

Sen, Amartya. 2002. *Rationality and Freedom*. Harvard University Press.

Sherburne, Donald W. 1957/1981. *A Key to Whitehead's Process and Reality*, The University of Chicago.

Simmel, Georg. 1978/2004. *The Philosophy of Money*, Routledge.

Veltman, Martinus. 2003. *Facts and Mysteries in Elementary Particle Physics*. World Scientifics Publishing Co. Pte. Ltd.

Von Mises, Ludwig. 1966. *Human Action: A Treatise on Economics*, Henery Regnery Company, third revised edition.

✓ Von Mises, Ludwig (author), Ebeling, Richard M. (editor). 1990. *Money, Method, and the Market Process: Essays by Ludwig Von Mises*, Springer.

ℳ Von Mises, Ludwig. 1912/2010. *The Theory of Money and Credit*, Pacific Publishing Studio.

Von Neumann John and Morgenstern, Oskar. 1944/2007. *Theory of Games and Economic Behavior*, Princeton University Press.

Wang, Zhengxing. 2003. *Principles of Quantum Mechanics*, Beking University Press.

Watson, Andrew. 2004. *The Quantum Quark*, Cambridge University Press.

Weinberg, Steven. 2003. *The Discovery of Subatomic Particles*, Cambridge University Press.

✓ Weinberg, Steven. 1992/2007. *Dreams of a Final Theory*, Human Science & Technology Press.

✓ Weyl Hermann. 1952/1983. *Symmetry*, Princeton University Press.

✓ Wheeler, John Archibald. 1990. *A Journey into Gravity and Spacetime*, Scientific American Library.

✓ Whitehead, Alfred North. 1938/1968. *Modes of Thought*, The Free Press.

Whitehead, Alfred North (author), Griffin, David Ray & Sherburne, Donald W. (editors of the corrected edition). 1978. *Process and Reality: An essay in Cosmology (Gifford Lectures Delivered in the University of Edinburgh During the Session 1927–1928)*, The Free Press.

Whitehead, Alfred North and Russell, Bertrand. 1923/2010. *Principia Mathematica*, Nabu Press

Wilczek, Frank. 2008. *The Lightness of Being: Mass, Ether, and the Unification of Forces*. Basic Books.

Wittgenstein,   Ludwig.   1969/1991.   *On   Certainty*, Wiley-Blackwell.

Yang, C.N. and Mills, R.L. 1954. Conservation of Isotopic Spin and Isotopic Gauge Invariance. *Physics Review, 96*, 191–5.

Yang, Y. 2006. "Toward a Mental Decision Logic of the Small-Grand World Problem: Its Decision Structure and Arithmatization." In Sun, R. & Miyake, N. (eds.), *Proceedings of the the Twenty-Eighth Annual Conference of the Cognitive Science Society*. Lawrence Erlbaum Associates.

Yang, Y., Braine, M. D. S., and O'Brien, D. 1998. "Some Empirical Justification of the Mental-predicate Logic Model." In Braine & O'Brien (eds.) *Mental Logic*, Lawrence Erlbaum Associates.

Yang, Y. and Johnson-Laird, P. N., 2000. "Illusions with Quantified Reasoning: How to Make the Impossible Seem Possible and Vice Versa," *Memory & Cognition*, Vol. 28 (3).

Yang, Y. and Johnson-Laird, P. N., 2000. "How to Eliminate Illusions in Quantified Reasoning." *Memory & Cognition*, Vol. 28 (6).

Zee, A. 1986/1999. *Fearful Symmetry*, Princeton University Press.

Zee, A. 2010. *Quantum Field Theory in a Nutshell*, Princeton University Press.

1 Auyang S
2 TD Lee
3 Weinberg S
4 A Zee
5 Wilczek F
6 Penrose R
7 Feynman R
8 R Healey
9 J A Wheeler
10 McMahon D / V. Icke

Index

Made in the USA
San Bernardino, CA
24 October 2013